MEDIEVAL

MEDIEVAL PEOPLE

EILEEN POWER, M.A., D.LIT.

DOUBLEDAY ANCHOR BOOKS

DOUBLEDAY & COMPANY, INC.

GARDEN CITY, NEW YORK

REPRINTED BY ARRANGEMENT WITH BARNES & NOBLE, INC.

DESIGN: JOSEPH P. ASCHERL

PRINTED IN THE UNITED STATES

For if heuene be on this erthe . and ese to any soule,
It is in cloistere or in scole . by many skilles I fynde;
For in cloistre cometh no man . to chide ne to fighte,
But alle is buxomnesse there and bokes . to rede and to
lerne,
In scole there is scorne . but if a clerke wil lerne,
And grete loue and lykynge . for eche of hem loueth other.

LANGLAND, *Piers Plowman*

Let us now praise famous men and our fathers that begat us. . . .

There be of them that have left a name behind them, that their praises might be reported.

And some there be which have no memorial; who are perished, as though they had never been; and are become as though they had never been born; and their children after them.

But these were merciful men, whose righteousness hath not been forgotten.

With their seed shall continually remain a good inheritance, and their children are within the covenant.

Their seed standeth fast, and their children for their sakes.

Their seed shall remain for ever, and their glory shall not be blotted out.

Their bodies are buried in peace; but their name liveth for evermore.

—Ecclesiasticus xliv.

PREFACE

SOCIAL HISTORY sometimes suffers from the reproach that it is vague and general, unable to compete with the attractions of political history either for the student or for the general reader, because of its lack of outstanding personalities. In point of fact there is often as much material for reconstructing the life of some quite ordinary person as there is for writing a history of Robert of Normandy or of Philippa of Hainault; and the lives of ordinary people so reconstructed are, if less spectacular, certainly not less interesting. I believe that social history lends itself particularly to what may be called a personal treatment, and that the past may be made to live again for the general reader more effectively by personifying it than by presenting it in the form of learned treatises on the development of the manor or on medieval trade, essential as these are to the specialist. For history, after all, is valuable only in so far as it lives, and Maeterlinck's cry, "There are no dead," should always be the historian's motto. It is the idea that history is about dead people, or, worse still, about movements and conditions which seem but vaguely related to the labours and passions of flesh and blood, which has driven history from bookshelves where the historical novel still finds a welcome place.

In the following series of sketches I have tried to illustrate at the same time various aspects of social life in the Middle Ages and various classes of historical material. Thus Bodo illustrates peasant life, and an early phase of a typical medieval estate; Marco Polo, Venetian trade with the East; Madame Eglentyne, monastic life; the Ménagier's wife, domestic life in a middle class home, and medieval ideas about women; Thomas Betson, the wool trade, and the activities of the great English trading company of Merchants of the Staple; and

Thomas Paycocke, the cloth industry in East Anglia. They are all quite ordinary people and unknown to fame, with the exception of Marco Polo. The types of historical evidence illustrated are the estate book of a manorial lord, the chronicle and traveller's tale, the bishop's register, the didactic treatise on household management, the collection of family letters, and houses, brasses and wills. At the end of the book I have added a bibliography of the sources which form the raw material for my reconstructions, and a few additional notes and references. I hope that this modest attempt to bring to life again some of "our fathers that begat us," may perhaps interest for an hour or two the general reader, or the teacher, who wishes to make more concrete by personification some of the general facts of medieval social and economic history.

My thanks are due to my publishers, Messrs. Methuen and Co. for allowing me to incorporate in Chapter VI the greater part of a chapter in my book "The Paycockes of Coggeshall," and to the Cambridge University Press for similarly allowing me to repeat in Chapter III a few sentences from my study of "Medieval English Nunneries." I have also to thank my friends Miss M. G. Jones and Miss H. M. R. Murray of Girton College, Cambridge, for various suggestions and criticisms, and my sister Miss Rhoda Power for making the index.

EILEEN POWER

London School of Economics and Political Science
University of London
May 1924

CONTENTS

MEDIEVAL PEOPLE

CHAPTER I

THE PEASANT BODO

Life on a Country Estate in the Time of Charlemagne

Three slender things that best support the world: the slender stream of milk from the cow's dug into the pail; the slender blade of green corn upon the ground; the slender thread over the hand of a skilled woman.

Three sounds of increase: the lowing of a cow in milk; the din of a smithy; the swish of a plough.

—From *The Triads of Ireland* (9th century)

ECONOMIC HISTORY, as we know it, is the newest of all the branches of history. Up to the middle of the last century the chief interest of the historian and of the public alike lay in political and constitutional history, in political events, wars, dynasties, and in political institutions and their development. Substantially, therefore, history concerned itself with the ruling classes. "Let us now praise famous men," was the historian's motto. He forgot to add "and our fathers that begat us." He did not care to probe the obscure lives and activities of the great mass of humanity, upon whose slow toil was built up the prosperity of the world and who were the hidden foundation of the political and constitutional edifice reared by the famous men he praised. To speak of ordinary people would have been beneath the dignity of history. Carlyle struck a significant note of revolt: "The thing I want to see," he said, "is not Red-book lists and Court Calendars and Parliamentary Registers, but the Life of Man in England: what men did, thought, suffered, enjoyed. . . . Mournful, in truth, it is to behold what the business called 'History' in these so enlightened and illuminated times still continues to be. Can you gather from it, read till your eyes go out, any dimmest shadow of an answer to that great question: How men lived and had

their being; were it but economically, as, what wages they got
and what they bought with these? Unhappily you cannot. . . .
History, as it stands all bound up in gilt volumes, is but a
shade more instructive than the wooden volumes of a back-
gammon-board."

Carlyle was a voice crying in the wilderness. Today the new
history, whose way he prepared, has come. The present age
differs from the centuries before it in its vivid realization of
that much-neglected person the man in the street; or (as it
was more often in the earliest ages) the man with the hoe.
To-day the historian is interested in the social life of the past
and not only in the wars and intrigues of princes. To the modern writer, the fourteenth century, for instance, is not merely
the century of the Hundred Years' War and of the Black
Prince and Edward III; more significantly it is for him the
era of the slow decay of villeinage in England, a fact more
epoch-making, in the long run, than the struggle over our
French provinces. We still praise famous men, for he would be
a poor historian who could spare one of the great figures who
have shed glory or romance upon the page of history; but we
praise them with due recognition of the fact that not only
great individuals, but people as a whole, unnamed and undis-
tinguished masses of people, now sleeping in unknown graves,
have also been concerned in the story. Our fathers that begat
us have come to their own at last. As Acton put it, "The
great historian now takes his meals in the kitchen."

This book is chiefly concerned with the kitchens of History,
and the first which we shall visit is a country estate at the
beginning of the ninth century. It so happens that we know a
surprising amount about such an estate, partly because Charlemagne himself issued a set of orders instructing the Royal
stewards how to manage his own lands, telling them everything it was necessary for them to know, down to the vegetables which they were to plant in the garden. But our chief
source of knowledge is a wonderful estate book which Irminon,
the Abbot of St. Germain des Prés near Paris, drew up so
that the abbey might know exactly what lands belonged to it
and who lived on those lands, very much as William I drew up

an estate book of his whole kingdom and called it "Domesday Book." In this estate book is set down the name of every little estate (or *fisc* as it was called) belonging to the abbey, with a description of the land which was worked under its steward to its own profit, and the land which was held by tenants, and the names of those tenants and of their wives and of their children, and the exact services and rents, down to a plank and an egg, which they had to do for their land. We know to-day the name of almost every man, woman, and child who was living on those little *fiscs* in the time of Charlemagne, and a great deal about their daily lives.

Consider for a moment how the estate upon which they lived was organized. The lands of the Abbey of St. Germain were divided into a number of estates, called *fiscs*, each of a convenient size to be administered by a steward. On each of these *fiscs* the land was divided into seigniorial and tributary lands; the first administered by the monks through a steward or some other officer, and the second possessed by various tenants, who received and held them from the abbey. These tributary lands were divided into numbers of little farms, called manses, each occupied by one or more families. If you had paid a visit to the chief or seigniorial manse, which the monks kept in their own hands, you would have found a little house, with three or four rooms, probably built of stone, facing an inner court, and on one side of it you would have seen a special group of houses hedged round, where the women serfs belonging to the house lived and did their work; all round you would also have seen little wooden houses, where the household serfs lived, workrooms, a kitchen, a bakehouse, barns, stables, and other farm buildings, and round the whole a hedge carefully planted with trees, so as to make a kind of enclosure or court. Attached to this central manse was a considerable amount of land—ploughland, meadows, vineyards, orchards and almost all the woods or forests on the estate. Clearly a great deal of labour would be needed to cultivate all these lands. Some of that labour was provided by servile workers, who were attached to the chief manse and lived in the court. But these household serfs were not nearly enough to do all the work upon the monks' land, and far the greater part of it had to be done by services paid by the other land-owners on the estate.

Beside the seigniorial manse, there were a number of little dependent manses. These belonged to men and women who were in various stages of freedom, except for the fact that all had to do work on the land of the chief manse. There is no need to trouble with the different classes, for in practice there was very little difference between them, and in a couple of centuries they were all merged into one common class of medieval villeins. The most important people were those called *coloni*, who were personally free (that is to say, counted as free men by the law), but bound to the soil, so that they could never leave their farms and were sold with the estate, if it were sold. Each of the dependent manses was held either by one family or by two or three families which clubbed together to do the work; it consisted of a house or houses, and farm buildings, like those of the chief manse, only poorer and made of wood, with ploughland and a meadow and perhaps a little piece of vineyard attached to it. In return for these holdings the owner or joint owners of every manse had to do work on the land of the chief manse for about three days in the week. The steward's chief business was to see that they did their work properly, and from every one he had the right to demand two kinds of labour. The first was *field work*: every year each man was bound to do a fixed amount of ploughing on the domain land (as it was called later on), and also to give what was called a *corvée*, that is to say, an unfixed amount of plough-ing, which the steward could demand every week when it was needed; the distinction corresponds to the distinction between *week work* and *boon work* in the later Middle Ages. The second kind of labour which every owner of a farm had to do on the monks' land was called handwork, that is to say, he had to help repair buildings, or cut down trees, or gather fruit, or make ale, or carry loads—anything, in fact, which wanted doing and which the steward told him to do. It was by these services that the monks got their own seigniorial farm cultivated. On all the other days of the week these hard-worked tenants were free to cultivate their own little farms, and we may be sure that they put twice as much elbow grease into the business.

But their obligation did not end here, for not only had they to pay services, they also had to pay certain rents to the big house. There were no State taxes in those days, but every man had to pay an army due, which Charlemagne exacted from the abbey, and which the abbey exacted from its tenants; this took the form of an ox and a certain number of sheep, or the equivalent in money: "He pays to the host two shillings of silver" comes first on every freeman's list of obligations. The farmers also had to pay in return for any special privileges granted to them by the monks; they had to carry a load of wood to the big house, in return for being allowed to gather firewood in the woods, which were jealously preserved for the use of the abbey; they had to pay some hogsheads of wine for the right to pasture their pigs in the same precious woods; every third year they had to give up one of their sheep for the right to graze upon the fields of the chief manse, they had to pay a sort of poll-tax of 4d. a head. In addition to these special rents every farmer had also to pay other rents in produce; every year he owed the big house three chickens and fifteen eggs and a large number of planks, to repair its buildings; often he had to give it a couple of pigs; sometimes corn, wine, honey, wax, soap, or oil. If the farmer were also an artisan and made things, he had to pay the produce of his craft; a smith would have to make lances for the abbey's contingent to the army, a carpenter had to make barrels and hoops and vine props, a wheelwright had to make a cart. Even the wives of the farmers were kept busy, if they happened to be serfs; for the servile women were obliged to spin cloth or to make a garment for the big house every year.

All these things were exacted and collected by the steward, whom they called *Villicus*, or *Major* (Mayor). He was a very hard-worked man, and when one reads the seventy separate and particular injunctions which Charlemagne addressed to his stewards one cannot help feeling sorry for him. He had to get all the right services out of the tenants, and tell them what to do each week and see that they did it; he had to be careful that they brought the right number of eggs and pigs up to the house, and did not foist off warped or badly planed planks upon him. He had to look after the household serfs too, and set them to work. He had to see about storing, or selling, or sending off to the monastery the produce of the estate and of the tenants' rents; and every year he had to present a full and detailed account of his stewardship to the abbot. He had a manse of his own, with services and rents due from it, and Charlemagne exhorted his stewards to be prompt in their payments, so as to set a good example. Probably his official duties left him very little time to work on his own farm, and he would have to put in a man to work it for him, as Charlemagne bade his stewards do. Often, however, he had subordinate officials called *deans* under him, and sometimes the work of receiving and looking after the stores in the big house was done by a special cellarer.

That, in a few words, is the way in which the monks of St. Germain and the other Frankish landowners of the time of Charlemagne managed their estates. Let us try, now, to look at those estates from a more human point of view and see what life was like to a farmer who lived upon them. The abbey possessed a little estate called Villaris, near Paris, in the place now occupied by the park of Saint Cloud. When we turn up the pages in the estate book dealing with Villaris, we find that there was a man called Bodo living there.[1] He had a wife called Ermentrude and three children called Wido and Gerbert and Hildegard; and he owned a little farm of arable and meadow land, with a few vines. And we know very nearly as much about Bodo's work as we know about that of a smallholder in France to-day. Let us try and imagine a day in his life. On a fine spring morning towards the end of Charlemagne's reign Bodo gets up early, because it is his day to go and work on the monks' farm, and he does not dare to be late, for fear of the steward. To be sure, he has probably given the steward a present of eggs and vegetables the week before, to keep him in a good temper; but the monks will not allow their stewards to take big bribes (as is sometimes done on other estates), and Bodo knows that he will not be allowed to go late to work. It is his day to plough, so he takes his big ox with him and little Wido to run by its side with a goad, and he joins his friends from some of the farms near by, who are going to work at the big house too. They all assemble, some with horses and oxen, some with mattocks and hoes and spades and axes and scythes, and go off in gangs to work upon the fields and meadows and woods of the seigniorial manse, according as the steward orders them. The manse next door to Bodo is held by a group of families: Frambert and Ermoin and Ragenold, with their wives and children. Bodo bids them good morning as he passes. Frambert is going to make a fence round the wood, to prevent the rabbits from coming out and eating the young crops; Ermoin has been told off to cart a great load of firewood up to the house; and Ragenold is mending a hole in the roof of a barn. Bodo goes whistling off in the cold with his oxen and his little boy; and it is no use to follow him farther, because he ploughs all day and eats his meal under a tree with the other ploughmen, and it is very monotonous.

Let us go back and see what Bodo's wife, Ermentrude, is doing. She is busy too; it is the day on which the chicken-rent is due—a fat pullet and five eggs in all. She leaves her second son, aged nine, to look after the baby Hildegard and calls on one of her neighbours, who has to go up to the big house too. The neighbour is a serf and she has to take the steward a piece of woollen cloth, which will be sent away to St. Germain to make a habit for a monk. Her husband is working all day in the lord's vineyards, for on this estate the serfs generally tend the vines, while the freemen do most of the ploughing. Ermentrude and the serf's wife go together up to the house. There all is busy. In the men's workshop are several clever workmen—a shoemaker, a carpenter, a blacksmith, and two silversmiths; there are not more, because the best artisans on the estates of St. Germain live by the walls of the abbey, so that they can work for the monks on the spot and save the labour of carriage. But there were always some craftsmen on every estate, either attached as serfs to the big house, or living on manses of their own, and good landowners tried to have as many clever craftsmen as possible.

Charlemagne ordered his stewards each to have in his district "good workmen, namely, blacksmiths, goldsmiths, silver-smiths, shoemakers, turners, carpenters, swordmakers, fisher-men, foilers, soapmakers, men who know how to make beer, cider, perry and all other kinds of beverages, bakers to make pasty for our table, netmakers who know how to make nets for hunting, fishing and fowling, and others too many to be named." [2] And some of these workmen are to be found work-ing for the monks in the estate of Villaris.

But Ermentrude does not stop at the men's workshop. She finds the steward, bobs her curtsy to him, and gives up her fowl and eggs, and then she hurries off to the women's part of the house, to gossip with the serfs there. The Franks used at this time to keep the women of their household in a separate quarter, where they did the work which was considered suit-able for women, very much as the Greeks of antiquity used to do. If a Frankish noble had lived at the big house, his wife would have looked after their work, but as no one lived in the stone house at Villaris, the steward had to oversee the women. Their quarter consisted of a little group of houses, with a work-room, the whole surrounded by a thick hedge with a strong bolted gate, like a harem, so that no one could come in with-out leave. Their workrooms were comfortable places, warmed by stoves, and there Ermentrude (who, being a woman, was allowed to go in) found about a dozen servile women spinning and dyeing cloth and sewing garments. Every week the harassed steward brought them the raw materials for their work and took away what they made. Charlemagne gives his stewards several instructions about the women attached to his manses, and we may be sure that the monks of St. Germain did the same on their model estates. "For our women's work," says Charlemagne, "they are to give at the proper time the materials, that is linen, wool, woad, vermilion, madder, wool combs, teasels, soap, grease, vessels, and other objects which are necessary. And let our women's quarters be well looked after, furnished with houses and rooms with stoves and cellars, and let them be surrounded by good hedge, and let the doors be strong, so that the women can do our work properly." [3]

Ermentrude, however, has to hurry away after her gossip, and so must we. She goes back to her own farm and sets to work in the little vineyard; then after an hour or two goes back to get the children's meal and to spend the rest of the day in weaving warm woollen clothes for them. All her friends are either working in the fields on their husband's farms or else looking after the poultry, or the vegetables, or sewing at home; for the women have to work just as hard as the men on a country farm. In Charlemagne's time (for instance) they did nearly all the sheep shearing. Then at last Bodo comes back for his supper, and as soon as the sun goes down they go to bed; for their hand-made candle gives only a flicker of light, and they both have to be up early in the morning. De Quincey once pointed out, in his inimitable manner, how the ancients everywhere went to bed, "like good boys, from seven to nine o'clock." "Man went to bed early in those ages simply because his worthy mother earth could not afford him candles. She, good old lady . . . would certainly have shuddered to hear of any of her nations asking for candles. 'Candles, indeed!' she would have said; 'who ever heard of such a thing? and with so much excellent daylight running to waste, as I have provided *gratis!* What will the wretches want next?' " [4] Something of the same situation prevailed even in Bodo's time.

This, then, is how Bodo and Ermentrude usually passed their working day. But, it may be complained, this is all very well. We know about the estates on which these peasants lived and about the rents which they had to pay, and the services which they had to do. But how did they feel and think and amuse themselves when they were not working? Rents and services are only outside things; an estate book only describes routine. It would be idle to try to picture the life of a university from a study of its lecture list, and it is equally idle to try and describe the life of Bodo from the estate book of his masters. It is no good taking your meals in the kitchen if you never talk to the servants. This is true, and to arrive at Bodo's thoughts and feelings and holiday amusements we must bid good-bye to Abbot Irminon's estate book, and peer into some very dark corners indeed; for though by the aid

of Chaucer and Langland and a few Court Rolls it is possible
to know a great deal about the feelings of a peasant six centuries later, material is scarce in the ninth century, and it is
all the more necessary to remember the secret of the invisible
ink.

Bodo certainly *had* plenty of feelings, and very strong ones.
When he got up in the frost on a cold morning to drive the
plough over the abbot's acres, when his own were calling out for
work, he often shivered and shook the rime from his beard,
and wished that the big house and all its land were at the bot-
tom of the sea (which, as a matter of fact, he had never seen
and could not imagine). Or else he wished he were the abbot's
huntsman, hunting in the forest; or a monk of St. Germain,
singing sweetly in the abbey church; or a merchant, taking
bales of cloaks and girdles along the high road to Paris; anything, in fact, but a poor ploughman ploughing other people's
land. An Anglo-Saxon writer has imagined a dialogue with
him:

"Well, ploughman, how do you do your work?" "Oh, sir,
I work very hard. I go out in the dawning, driving the oxen to
the field and I yoke them to the plough. Be the winter never so
stark, I dare not stay at home for fear of my lord; but every
day I must plough a full acre or more, after having yoked the
oxen and fastened the share and coulter to the plough!" "Have
you any mate?" "I have a boy, who drives the oxen with a
goad, who is now hoarse from cold and shouting." (Poor
little Wido!) "Well, well, it is very hard work?" "Yes, indeed
it is very hard work." [5]

Nevertheless, hard as the work was, Bodo sang lustily to
cheer himself and Wido; for is it not related that once, when a
clerk was singing the "Allelulia" in the emperor's presence,
Charles turned to one of the bishops, saying, "My clerk is
singing very well," whereat the rude bishop replied, "Any clown
in our countryside drones as well as that to his oxen at their
ploughing"? [6] It is certain too that Bodo agreed with the names
which the great Charles gave to the months of the year in his
own Frankish tongue; for he called January "Winter-month,"

February "Mud-month," March "Spring-month," April "Easter-month," May "Joy-month," June "Plough-month," July "Hay-month," August "Harvest-month," September "Wind-month," October "Vintage-month," November "Autumn-month," and December "Holy-month." [7]

And Bodo was a superstitious creature. The Franks had been Christian now for many years, but Christian though they were, the peasant clung to old beliefs and superstitions. On the estates of the holy monks of St. Germain you would have found the country people saying charms which were hoary with age, parts of the lay sung by the Frankish ploughman over his bewitched land long before he marched southwards into the Roman Empire, or parts of the spell which the bee-master performed when he swarmed his bees on the shores of the Baltic Sea. Christianity has coloured these charms, but it has not effaced their heathen origin; and because the tilling of the soil is the oldest and most unchanging of human occupations, old beliefs and superstitions cling to it and the old gods stalk up and down the brown furrows, when they have long vanished from houses and roads. So on Abbot Irminon's estates the peasant-farmers muttered charms over their sick cattle (and over their sick children too) and said incantations over the fields to make them fertile. If you had followed behind Bodo when he broke his first furrow you would have probably seen him take out of his jerkin a little cake, baked for him by Ermentrude out of different kinds of meal, and you would have seen him stoop and lay it under the furrow and sing:

> Earth, Earth, Earth! O Earth, our mother!
> May the All-Wielder, Ever-Lord grant thee
> Acres a-waxing, upwards a-growing,
> Pregnant with corn and plenteous in strength;
> Hosts of grain shafts and of glittering plants!
> Of broad barley the blossoms,
> And of white wheat ears waxing,
> Of the whole land the harvest. . . .

Acre, full-fed, bring forth fodder for men!
Blossoming brightly, blessed become!
And the God who wrought with earth grant us gift of growing
That each of all the corns may come unto our need.[8]

Then he would drive his plough through the acre.

The Church wisely did not interfere with these old rites. It taught Bodo to pray to the Ever-Lord instead of to Father Heaven, and to the Virgin Mary instead of to Mother Earth, and with these changes let the old spell he had learned from his ancestors serve him still. It taught him, for instance, to call on Christ and Mary in his charm for bees. When Ermentrude heard her bees swarming, she stood outside her cottage and said this little charm over them:

> Christ, there is a swarm of bees outside,
> Fly hither, my little cattle,
> In blest peace, in God's protection,
> Come home safe and sound.
> Sit down, sit down, bee,
> St. Mary commanded thee.
> Thou shalt not have leave,
> Thou shalt not fly to the wood.
> Thou shalt not escape me,
> Nor go away from me.
> Sit very still,
> Wait God's will! [9]

And if Bodo on his way home saw one of his bees caught in a brier bush, he immediately stood still and wished—as some people wish to-day when they go under a ladder. It was the Church, too, which taught Bodo to add "So be it, Lord," to the end of his charm against pain. Now, his ancestors for generations behind him had believed that if you had a stitch in your side, or a bad pain anywhere, it came from a worm in the marrow of your bones, which was eating you up, and that the only way to get rid of that worm was to put a knife, or an arrow-head, or some other piece of metal to the sore place, and then wheedle the worm out on to the blade by saying a

charm. And this was the charm which Bodo's heathen ancestors had always said and which Bodo went on saying when
little Wido had a pain: "Come out, worm, with nine little
worms, out from the marrow into the bone, from the bone
into the flesh, from the flesh into the skin, from the skin into
this arrow." And then (in obedience to the Church) he added
"So be it, Lord." [10] But sometimes it was not possible to read
a Christian meaning into Bodo's doings. Sometimes he paid
visits to some man who was thought to have a wizard's powers,
or superstitiously reverenced some twisted tree, about which
were hung old stories never quite forgotten. Then the Church
was stern. When he went to confession the priest would ask
him: "Have you consulted magicians and enchanters, have
you made vows to trees and fountains, have you drunk any
magic philtre?" [11] And he would have to confess what he did
last time his cow was sick. But the Church was kind as
well as stern. "When serfs come to you," we find one
bishop telling his priests, "you must not give them as
many fasts to perform as rich men. Put upon them only half
the penance." [12] The Church knew well enough that Bodo
could not drive his plough all day upon an empty stomach.
The hunting, drinking, feasting Frankish nobles could afford to
lose a meal.

It was from this stern and yet kind Church that Bodo got
his holidays. For the Church made the pious emperor decree
that on Sundays and saints' days no servile or other works
should be done. Charlemagne's son repeated his decree in
827. It runs thus:

We ordain according to the law of God and to the command
of our father of blessed memory in his edicts, that no servile
works shall be done on Sundays, neither shall men perform
their rustic labours, tending vines, ploughing fields, reaping
corn and mowing hay, setting up hedges or fencing woods,
cutting trees, or working in quarries or building houses; nor
shall they work in the garden, nor come to the law courts, nor
follow the chase. But three carrying-services it is lawful to do
on Sunday, to wit carrying for the army, carrying food, or

carrying (if need be) the body of a lord to its grave. Item,
women shall not do their textile works, nor cut out clothes,
nor stitch them together with the needle, nor card wool, nor
beat hemp, nor wash clothes in public, nor shear sheep: so
that there may be rest on the Lord's day. But let them come
together from all sides to Mass in the Church and praise God
for all the good things He did for us on that day! [13]

Unfortunately, however, Bodo and Ermentrude and their
friends were not content to go quietly to church on saints'
days and quietly home again. They used to spend their holidays in dancing and singing and buffoonery, as country folk
have always done until our own gloomier, more self-conscious
age. They were very merry and not at all refined, and the place
they always chose for their dances was the churchyard; and
unluckily the songs they sang as they danced in a ring were
old pagan songs of their forefathers, left over from old May-
day festivities, which they could not forget, or ribald love-
songs which the Church disliked. Over and over again we find
the Church councils complaining that the peasants (and sometimes the priests too) were singing "wicked songs with a
chorus of dancing women," or holding "ballads and dancings
and evil and wanton songs and such-like lures of the devil";[14]
over and over again the bishops forbade these songs and
dances; but in vain. In every country in Europe, right through
the Middle Ages to the time of the Reformation, and after
it, country folk continued to sing and dance in the churchyard. Two hundred years after Charlemagne's death there
grew up the legend of the dancers of Kölbigk, who danced on
Christmas Eve in the churchyard, in spite of the warning of
the priest, and all got rooted to the spot for a year, till the
Archbishop of Cologne released them. Some men say that
they were not rooted standing to the spot, but that they had
to go on dancing for the whole year; and that before they were
released they had danced themselves waist-deep into the
ground. People used to repeat the little Latin verse which they
were singing:

Equitabat Bovo per silvam frondosam
Ducebat sibi Merswindem formosam.
Quid stamus? Cur non imus? [15]

Through the leafy forest, Bovo went a-riding
And his pretty Merswind trotted on beside him—
Why are we standing still? Why can't we go away?

Another later story still is told about a priest in Worcester-
shire, who was kept awake all night by the people dancing
in his churchyard and singing a song with the refrain "Sweetheart have pity," so that he could not get it out of his head,
and the next morning at Mass, instead of saying "Dominus
vobiscum," he said "Sweetheart have pity," and there was a
dreadful scandal which got into a chronicle.[16]

Sometimes our Bodo did not dance himself, but listened
to the songs of wandering minstrels. The priests did not at
all approve of these minstrels, who (they said) would certainly go to hell for singing profane secular songs, all about
the great deeds of heathen heroes of the Frankish race, instead
of Christian hymns. But Bodo loved them, and so did Bodo's
betters; the Church councils had sometimes even to rebuke
abbots and abbesses for listening to their songs. And the worst
of it was that the great emperor himself, the good Charlemagne, loved them too. He would always listen to a minstrel,
and his biographer, Einhard, tells us that "He wrote out the
barbarous and ancient songs, in which the acts of the kings
and their wars were sung, and committed them to memory";[17] and one at least of those old sagas, which he liked men
to write down, has been preserved on the cover of a Latin
manuscript, where a monk scribbled it in his spare time. His
son, Louis the Pious, was very different; he rejected the national poems, which he had learnt in his youth, and would
not have them read or recited or taught; he would not allow
minstrels to have justice in the law courts, and he forbade idle
dances and songs and tales in public places on Sundays; but
then he also dragged down his father's kingdom into disgrace
and ruin. The minstrels repaid Charlemagne for his kindness
to them. They gave him everlasting fame; for all through the

Middle Ages the legend of Charlemagne grew, and he shares
with our King Arthur the honour of being the hero of one of
the greatest romance-cycles of the Middle Ages. Every different century clad him anew in its own dress and sang new lays
about him. What the monkish chroniclers in their cells could
never do for Charlemagne, these despised and accursed minstrels did for him: they gave him what is perhaps more desirable and more lasting than a place in history—they gave him
a place in legend. It is not every emperor who rules in those
realms of gold of which Keats spoke, as well as in the kingdoms
of the world; and in the realms of gold Charlemagne reigns
with King Arthur, and his peers joust with the Knights of the
Round Table. Bodo, at any rate, benefited by Charles's love
of minstrels, and it is probable that he heard in the lifetime of
the emperor himself the first beginnings of those legends
which afterwards clung to the name of Charlemagne. One
can imagine him round-eyed in the churchyard, listening to
fabulous stories of Charles's Iron March to Pavia, such as a
gossiping old monk of St. Gall afterwards wrote down in his
chronicle.[18]

It is likely enough that such legends were the nearest Bodo
ever came to seeing the emperor, of whom even the poor
serfs who never followed him to court or camp were proud.
But Charles was a great traveller: like all the monarchs of the
early Middle Ages he spent the time, when he was not warring,
in trekking round his kingdom, staying at one of his estates,
until he and his household had literally eaten their way
through it, and then passing on to another. And sometimes he
varied the procedure by paying a visit to the estates of his
bishops or nobles, who entertained him royally. It may be
that one day he came on a visit to Bodo's masters and stopped
at the big house on his way to Paris, and then Bodo saw him
plain; for Charlemagne would come riding along the road in
his jerkin of otter skin, and his plain blue cloak (Einhard
tells us that he hated grand clothes and on ordinary days
dressed like the common people);[19] and after him would
come his three sons and his bodyguard, and then his five
daughters. Einhard has also told us that

He had such care of the upbringing of his sons and daughters that he never dined without them when he was at home and never travelled without them. His sons rode along with him and his daughters followed in the rear. Some of his guards, chosen for this very purpose, watched the end of the line of march where his daughters travelled. They were very beautiful and much beloved by their father, and, therefore, it is strange that he would give them in marriage to no one, either among his own people or of a foreign state. But up to his death he kept them all at home saying he could not forgo their society.[20]

Then, with luck, Bodo, quaking at the knees, might even behold a portent new to his experience, the emperor's elephant. Haroun El Raschid, the great Sultan of the "Arabian Nights" had sent it to Charles, and it accompanied him on all his progresses. Its name was "Abu-Lubabah," which is an Arabic word and means "the father of intelligence," * and it died a hero's death on an expedition against the Danes in 810. It is certain that ever afterwards Ermentrude quelled little Gerbert, when he was naughty, with the threat, "Abu-Lubabah will come with his long nose and carry you off." But Wido, being aged eight and a bread-winner, professed to have felt no fear on being confronted with the elephant; but admitted when pressed, that he greatly preferred Haroun El Raschid's other present to the emperor, the friendly dog, who answered to the name of "Becerillo."

It would be a busy time for Bodo when all these great folk came, for everything would have to be cleaned before their arrival, the pastry cooks and sausage-makers summoned and a great feast prepared; and though the household serfs did most of the work, it is probable that he had to help. The gossipy old monk of St. Gall has given us some amusing pictures of the excitement when Charles suddenly paid a visit to his subjects:

* *Abu-Lubabah.*—It is remarkable that the name should have suffered no corruption in the chronicles.

There was a certain bishopric which lay full in Charles's path when he journeyed, and which indeed he could hardly avoid: and the bishop of this place, always anxious to give satisfaction, put everything that he had at Charles's disposal. But once the Emperor came quite unexpectedly and the bishop in great anxiety had to fly hither and thither like a swallow, and had not only the palaces and houses but also the courts and squares swept and cleaned: and then, tired and irritated, came to meet him. The most pious Charles noticed this, and after examining all the various details, he said to the bishop: "My kind host, you always have everything splendidly cleaned for my arrival." Then the bishop, as if divinely inspired, bowed his head and grasped the king's never-conquered right hand, and hiding his irritation, kissed it and said: "It is but right, my lord, that, wherever you come, all things should be thoroughly cleansed." Then Charles, of all kings the wisest, understanding the state of affairs said to him: "If I empty I can also fill." And he added: "You may have that estate which lies close to your bishopric, and all your successors may have it until the end of time." In the same journey, too, he came to a bishop who lived in a place through which he must needs pass. Now on that day, being the sixth day of the week, he was not willing to eat the flesh of beast or bird; and the bishop, being by reason of the nature of the place unable to procure fish upon the sudden, ordered some excellent cheese, rich and creamy, to be placed before him. And the most self-restrained Charles, with the readiness which he showed everywhere and on all occasions, spared the blushes of the bishop and required no better fare; but taking up his knife cut off the skin, which he thought unsavoury and fell to on the white of the cheese. Thereupon the bishop, who was standing near like a servant, drew closer and said: "Why do you do that, lord emperor? You are throwing away the very best part." Then Charles, who deceived no one, and did not believe that anyone would deceive him, on the persuasion of the bishop put a piece of the skin in his mouth, and slowly eat it and swallowed it like butter. Then approving of the advice of the bishop, he said:

"Very true, my good host," and he added: "Be sure to send me every year to Aix two cartloads of just such cheeses." And the bishop was alarmed at the impossibility of the task and, fearful of losing both his rank and his office, he rejoined: "My lord, I can procure the cheeses, but I cannot tell which are of this quality and which of another. Much I fear lest I fall under your censure." Then Charles, from whose penetration and skill nothing could escape, however new or strange it might be, spoke thus to the bishop, who from childhood had known such cheeses and yet could not test them: "Cut them in two," he said, "Then fasten together with a skewer those that you find to be of the right quality and keep them in your cellar for a time and then send them to me. The rest you may keep for yourself and your clergy and your family." This was done for two years, and the king ordered the present of cheeses to be taken in without remark: then in the third year the bishop brought in person his laboriously collected cheeses. But the most just Charles pitied his labour and anxiety and added to the bishopric an excellent estate whence he and his successors might provide themselves with corn and wine.[22]

We may feel sorry for the poor flustered bishop collecting his two cartloads of cheeses; but it is possible that our real sympathy ought to go to Bodo, who probably had to pay an extra rent in cheeses to satisfy the emperor's taste, and got no excellent estate to recompense him.

A visit from the emperor, however, would be a rare event in his life, to be talked about for years and told to his grandchildren. But there was one other event, which happened annually, and which was certainly looked for with excitement by Bodo and his friends. For once a year the king's itinerant justices, the *Missi Dominici*, came round to hold their court and to see if the local counts had been doing justice. Two of them would come, a bishop and a count, and they would perhaps stay a night at the big house as guests of the abbot, and the next day they would go on to Paris, and there they would sit and do justice in the open square before the church, and from all the district round great men and small, nobles and freemen and *coloni*, would bring their grievances and demand redress. Bodo would go too, if anyone had injured or robbed him, and would make his complaint to the judges. But if he were canny he would not go to them empty-handed, trusting to justice alone. Charlemagne was very strict, but unless the *missi* were exceptionally honest and pious they would not be averse to taking bribes. Theodulf, Bishop of Orleans, who was one of the Emperor's *missi*, has left us a most entertaining Latin poem, in which he describes the attempts of the clergy and laymen, who flocked to his court, to buy justice.[23] Every one according to his means brought a present; the rich offered money, precious stones, fine materials, and Eastern carpets, arms, horses, antique vases of gold or silver chiselled with representations of the labours of Hercules. The poor brought skins of Cordova leather, tanned and untanned, excellent pieces of cloth and linen (poor Ermentrude must have worked hard for the month before the justices came!), boxes, and wax. "With this battering-ram," cries the shocked Bishop Theodulf, "they hope to break down the wall of my soul. But they would not have thought that they could shake *me*, if they had not so shaken other judges before." And indeed, if his picture be true, the royal justices must have been followed about by a regular caravan of carts and horses to carry their presents. Even Theodulf has to admit that, in order not to hurt people's feelings, he was obliged to accept certain unconsidered trifles in the shape of eggs and bread and wine and chickens and little birds, "whose bodies" (he says, smacking his lips) "are small, but very good to eat." One seems to detect the anxious face of Bodo behind those eggs and little birds.

Another treat Bodo had which happened once a year; for regularly on the ninth of October there began the great fair of St. Denys, which went on for a whole month, outside the gate of Paris.[24] Then for a week before the fair little booths and sheds sprang up, with open fronts in which the merchants could display their wares, and the Abbey of St. Denys, which had the right to take a toll of all the merchants who came

there to sell, saw to it that the fair was well enclosed with
fences, and that all came in by the gates and paid their money,
for wily merchants were sometimes known to burrow under
fences or climb over them so as to avoid the toll. Then the
streets of Paris were crowded with merchants bringing their
goods, packed in carts and upon horses and oxen; and on the
opening day all regular trade in Paris stopped for a month,
and every Parisian shopkeeper was in a booth somewhere in
the fair, exchanging the corn and wine and honey of the district for rarer goods from foreign parts. Bodo's abbey probably
had a stall in the fair and sold some of those pieces of cloth
woven by the serfs in the women's quarter, or cheeses and
salted meat prepared on the estates, or wine paid in rent by
Bodo and his fellow-farmers. Bodo would certainly take a holiday and go to the fair. In fact, the steward would probably
have great difficulty in keeping his men at work during the
month; Charlemagne had to give a special order to his stewards that they should "be careful that our men do properly
the work which it is lawful to exact from them, and that
they do not waste their time in running about to markets
and fairs." Bodo and Ermentrude and the three children,
all attired in their best, did not consider it waste of time
to go to the fair even twice or three times. They pretended
that they wanted to buy salt to salt down their winter meat,
or some vermilion dye to colour a frock for the baby. What
they really wanted was to wander along the little rows of
booths and look at all the strange things assembled there;
for merchants came to St. Denys to sell their rich goods from
the distant East to Bodo's betters, and wealthy Frankish
nobles bargained there for purple and silken robes with orange
borders, stamped leather jerkins, peacock's feathers, and the
scarlet plumage of flamingos (which they called "phœnix
skins"), scents and pearls and spices, almonds and raisins, and
monkeys for their wives to play with.[25] Sometimes these merchants were Venetians, but more often they were Syrians or
crafty Jews, and Bodo and his fellows laughed loudly over the
story of how a Jewish merchant had tricked a certain bishop,
who craved for all the latest novelties, by stuffing a mouse

with spices and offering it for sale to him, saying that "he had brought this most precious never-before-seen animal from Judea," and refusing to take less than a whole measure of silver for it.[26] In exchange for their luxuries these merchants took away with them Frisian cloth, which was greatly esteemed, and corn and hunting dogs, and sometimes a piece of fine goldsmith's work, made in a monastic workshop. And Bodo would hear a hundred dialects and tongues, for men of Saxony and Frisia, Spain and Provence, Rouen and Lombardy, and perhaps an Englishman or two, jostled each other in the little streets; and from time to time there came also an Irish scholar with a manuscript to sell, and the strange, sweet songs of Ireland on his lips:

> A hedge of trees surrounds me,
> A blackbird's lay sings to me;
> Above my lined booklet
> The trilling birds chant to me.
>
> In a grey mantle from the top of bushes
> The cuckoo sings:
> Verily—may the Lord shield me!—
> Well do I write under the greenwood.[27]

Then there were always jugglers and tumblers, and men with performing bears, and minstrels to wheedle Bodo's few pence out of his pocket. And it would be a very tired and happy family that trundled home in the cart to bed. For it is not, after all, so dull in the kitchen, and when we have quite finished with the emperor, 'Charlemagne and all his peerage,' it is really worth while to spend a few moments with Bodo in his little manse. History is largely made up of Bodos.

CHAPTER II

MARCO POLO

A Venetian Traveller of the Thirteenth Century

Et por ce, veul ie que un et autre sachent a tos iors mais les euvres des Veneciens, et qui il furent, et dont il vindrent, et qui il sont, et comment il firent la noble Cite que l'en apele Venise, qui est orendroit la plus bele dou siecle. . . . La place de Monseignor Saint Marc est orendroit la plus bele place qui soit en tot li monde; que de vers li soleil levant est la plus bele yglise qui soit el monde, c'est l'Yglise de Monseignor Saint Marc. Et de les cele Yglise est li paleis de Monseignor li Dus, grant e biaus a mervoilles.

—MARTINO DA CANALE

And Kinsai [Hangchow] is the greatest city in the whole world, so great that I should scarcely venture to tell of it, but that I have met at Venice people in plenty who have been there. . . . And if anyone should desire to tell of all the vastness and great marvels of this city, a good quire of paper would not hold the matter, I trow. For 'tis the greatest and noblest city, and the finest for merchandise, that the whole world containeth.

—ODORIC OF PORDENONE

LET us go back in mind—as would that we could go back in body—to the year 1268. It is a year which makes no great stir in the history books, but it will serve us well. In those days, as in our own, Venice lay upon her lagoons, a city (as Cassiodorus long ago saw her*) like a sea-bird's nest afloat on the shallow waves, a city like a ship, moored to the land but only at home upon the seas, the proudest city in all the West-

---

* "Hic vobis, aquatilium avium more, domus est."

ern world. For only consider her position. Lying at the head of
the Adriatic, half-way between East and West, on the one
great sea thoroughfare of medieval commerce, a Mediterranean seaport, yet set so far north that she was almost in the
heart of Europe, Venice gathered into her harbour all the
trade routes overland and overseas, on which pack-horses could
travel or ships sail. Merchants bringing silk and spices, cam-
phor and ivory, pearls and scents and carpets from the Levant
and from the hot lands beyond it, all came to port in Venice.
For whether they came by way of Egypt sailing between the
low banks of the Nile and jolting on camels to Alexandria,
or whether they came through the rich and pleasant land of
Persia and the Syrian desert to Antioch and Tyre, or whether
they slowly pushed their way in a long, thin caravan across the
highlands of Central Asia and south of the Caspian Sea to
Trebizond, and so sailed through the Black Sea and the Darda-
nelles, Venice was their natural focus. Only Constantinople
might have rivalled her, and Constantinople she conquered.
To Venice, therefore, as if drawn by a magnet, came the
spoils of the East, and from Venice they went by horse across
the Alps by the Brenner and St. Gothard passes to Germany
and France, or in galleys by way of the Straits of Gibraltar
to England and Flanders; [1] and the galleys and pack-horses
came back again to Venice, laden with the metals of Germany,
the furs of Scandinavia, the fine wools of England, the cloth
of Flanders, and the wine of France.

But if geography gave Venice an unrivalled site, the Venetians did the rest. Through all the early years of their history
they defied Constantinople to the east of them, and Pope and
Holy Roman Emperor to the west; sometimes turning to one,
sometimes to the other, but stubbornly bent all the while
upon independence, replying, when invited to become subjects: "God, Who is our help and protector has saved us to
dwell upon these waters. This Venice, which we have raised
in the lagoons, is our mighty habitation, no power of emperor or of prince can touch us"; apt, if threatened, to retire
to their islands and derisively to fire cannon balls of bread
into the mainland force, which sought to starve them out.[2]

Always they were conscious that their future lay upon the
waters, and in that East, whose colour had crept into their
civilization and warmed their blood. They were Eastern and
Western both, the Venetians, hot hearts for loving and con-
quering, icy heads for scheming and ruling. Bit by bit they
secured the ring of mainland behind them, all the while keeping at bay the Saracen and Slav sea rovers, whose ships were
the terror of the Mediterranean. Then they descended upon
the pirates of Dalmatia, who thus harassed their trading vessels, and took all the Dalmatian coast. The Doge of Venice
became Duke of Dalmatia. "True it is," says their chronicler,
"that the Adriatic Sea is in the duchy of Venice," [3] and they
called it the "Gulf of Venice." Now it was that there was
first instituted the magnificent symbolical ceremony of wedding the sea, with the proud words "Desponsamus te mare in
signum veri perpetuique domini"! [4]

> She was a maiden city, bright and free,
> No guile seduced, no force could violate,
> And when she took unto herself a mate
> She must espouse the everlasting sea.

And truly it seemed as though the very sea had sworn to
honour and obey her.

Then came the Crusades, when Europe forgot its differ-
ences and threw itself upon the paynim who held the holy
places of its faith, when men from all lands marched behind
the banner of the Cross and the towers of Jerusalem were
more real than the Tower of Babel. Now, at last, Venice saw
her dream within her hand. It was Venice who provided galleys and Venice who provided convoys and commissariat and
soldiers, at a good round sum; and when time came for the
division of the spoil, Venice demanded in every captured
town of Palestine and Syria a church, a counting-house and
the right to trade without tolls. Her great chance came in the
Fourth Crusade, when her old blind Doge Enrico Dandolo
(whose blindness had the Nelson touch), upon the pretext
that the Crusaders could not pay the transport fees agreed
upon, turned the whole Crusade to the use of Venice, and

conquered first Zara, which had dared to revolt from her, and then her ancient—her only—rival, the immortal Byzantium itself. It is true that the Pope excommunicated the Venetians when they first turned the armies against Zara, but what matter? They looted Constantinople and brought back the four great gilded horses to St. Mark's—St. Mark's, which has been compared to a robbers' cave crowded with the booty of the Levant, and which held the sacred body of the saint, stolen from Alexandria by the Venetians, nearly four centuries before, concealed in a tub of pickled pork, in order to elude the Moslems. A Venetian patriarch now said Mass in St. Sophia. Venice received the proud title of "Ruler of a half and a quarter of the Roman Empire," ("quartæ partis et dimidiæ totius imperii Romaniæ"—the words have a ring of trumpets), and the Doge, buskined in scarlet like the ancient Roman emperors, now ruled supreme over four seas—the Adriatic, the Ægean, the Sea of Marmora, and the Black Sea. Venetian factories studded all the Levantine coasts, in Tripoli and Tyre, Salonica, Adrianople, and Constantinople, in Trebizond on the Black Sea, even at Caffa in the far Crimea, whence ran the mysterious road into Russia. Crete and Rhodes and Cyprus were hers; her galleys swept the pirates from the seas and brooked no rivals; all trade with the East must pass through Venice, and Venice only. The other trading cities of Italy struggled against her, and Genoa came near to rivalling her, but in 1258, and again in 1284, she utterly defeated the Genoese fleet. Not for the city of "sea without fish, mountains without woods, men without faith, and women without shame" was it to bit the horses on St. Mark's.[5] In 1268 Venice seemed supreme. Byzantium was her washpot and over the Levant she had cast her shoe. Truly her chronicler might write of her:

Dalmatia, Albania, Rumania, Greece, Trebizond, Syria, Armenia, Egypt, Cyprus, Candia, Apulia, Sicily, and other countries, kingdoms and islands were the fruitful gardens, the proud castles of our people, where they found again pleasure, profit, and security. . . . The Venetians went about the sea, here and there and across the sea, and in all places wheresoever water runs, and bought merchandise and brought it to Venice from every side. Then there came to Venice Germans and Bavarians, French and Lombards, Tuscans and Hungarians, and every people that lives by merchandise and they took it to their countries.

Small wonder that (as a later traveller observed) the Venetians were proud of their great rule, and when a son was born to a Venetian were wont to say among themselves, "A Signor is born into the world."

Is it not true to say that Venice was the proudest city on earth, *la noble cite que l'en apele Venise, qui est orendroit la plus bele dou siecle*? [6] Life was a fair and splendid thing for those merchant princes, who held the gorgeous East in fee in the year of grace 1268. In that year traders in great stone counting-houses, lapped by the waters of the canals, were checking, book in hand, their sacks of cloves, mace and nutmegs, cinnamon and ginger from the Indies, ebony chessmen from Indo China, ambergris from Madagascar, and musk from Tibet. In that year the dealers in jewels were setting prices upon diamonds from Golconda, rubies and lapis lazuli from Badakhshan, and pearls from the fisheries of Ceylon; and the silk merchants were stacking up bales of silk and muslin and brocade from Bagdad and Yezd and Malabar and China. In that year young gallants on the Rialto (scented gallants, but each, like Shakespeare's Antonio, with a ship venturing into port somewhere in the Levant) rubbed elbows with men of all nations, heard travellers' tales of all lands, and at dawn slipped along the canals in gondolas (not black in those days, but painted and hung with silk), saluting the morning with songs; and the red-haired ladies of Venice whom centuries later Titian loved to paint, went trailing up and down the marble steps of their palaces, with all the brocades of Persia on their backs and all the perfumes of Arabia to sweeten their little hands.

It was in that year, too, that one Martino da Canale, a clerk in the customs house, began to busy himself (like

Chaucer after him) less with his accounts than with writing
in the delectable French language ("por ce que lengue
franceise cort parmi le monde, et est la plus delitable a lire
et a oir que nule autre") a chronicle of Venice. It is of the
water, watery, Canale's chronicle, like Ariel's dirge; he has
indeed, "that intenseness of feeling which seems to resolve
itself into the elements which it contemplates." Here is nothing indeed, of "the surge and thunder of the Odyssey," but
the lovely words sparkle like the sun on the waters of the
Mediterranean, and like a refrain, singing itself in and out of
the narrative, the phrase recurs, "Li tens estoit clers et biaus
. . . et lors quant il furent en mer, li mariniers drecerent les
voiles au vent, et lesserent core a ploine voiles les mes parmi
la mer a la force dou vent";[7] for so much of the history of
Venice was enacted upon deck. It is a passing proud chronicle,
too, for Canale was, and well he knew it, a citizen of no mean
city

"Now would I," he says "that every one and all know
for ever the works of the Venetians, who they were and whence
they came and what they are, and how they made the noble
city which is called Venice, which is this day the fairest in
the world. And I would that all those who are now living and
those who are to come know how the noble city is builded and
how all good things abound in her, and how the sire of the
Venetians, the noble Doge, is powerful, and what nobility is
found therein and the prowess of the Venetian people, and
how they are all perfect in the faith of Jesu Christ and obedient to holy Church, and how they never disobey the commandment of holy Church. Within this noble Venice there
dares to dwell neither heretic, nor usurer, murderer, thief nor
robber. And I will tell you the names of all the Doges that
have been in Venice, one after the other, and what they did to
the honour of holy Church and of their noble City. And I will
tell you the names of the noble captains whom the noble
Doges sent in their time to lay low their enemies, and concerning the victories that they won I will have you know, for
it is fitting. . . . In the year of the incarnation of our Lord

Jesu Christ MCCLXVII years, in the time of Milord Renier
Zeno, the high Doge of Venice, I laboured and strove until
I found the ancient history of the Venetians, whence they
came first and how they builded the noble city called Venice,
which is to-day the fairest and the pleasantest in the world,
full of beauty and of all good things. Merchandise flows
through this noble city even as water flows from the fountains,
and the salt water runs through it and round it and in all
places save in the houses and the streets; and when the
citizens go abroad they can return to their houses by land or
by water, as they will. From all parts there come merchandise
and merchants, who buy merchandise as they will and take
it back to their own countries. Within this town is found food
in great plenty, bread and wine, land fowl and river fowl,
fresh meat and salt, and sea fish and river fish. . . . You may
find within this fair town many men of gentle birth, both old
men and young *damoisaus* in plenty, and merchants with
them, who buy and sell, and money changers and citizens of
all crafts, and therewith mariners of all sorts, and ships to
carry them to all lands and galleys to lay low their enemies.
And in this fair town is also great plenty of ladies and damsels
and maidens, very richly apparelled." [8]

It happened that there was a new Doge that year, our
year 1268, Lorenzo Tiepolo by name, and a great procession
of the gilds took place before the palace on the Piazza of
St. Mark to welcome his accession. Martino da Canale was
watching it and wrote it all down in his chronicle. First came
the navy sailing past in the harbour, fifty galleys and other
ships, with their crews cheering and shouting on deck. Then
came the gilds on foot: first the master smiths, with garlands
on their heads and banners and trumpets; then the furriers
apparelled in samite and scarlet silk, with mantles of ermine
and vair; then the weavers richly bedight, and the ten master
tailors in white with crimson stars. Then the master cloth-
workers passed, carrying boughs of olive and wearing crowns
of olive on their heads; then the fustian makers in furred robes
of their own weaving, and the quilt makers with garlands of

gilt beads and white cloaks sewn with fleurs-de-lis, marching
two by two, with little children singing *chansonettes* and
cobles before them. Then came the makers of cloth of gold, all
in cloth of gold, and their servants in cloth of gold or of purple,
followed by the mercers in silk and the butchers in scarlet, the
fish sellers robed and furred and garlanded, and the master bar-
bers, having with them two riders attired as knights-errant, and
four captive damsels, strangely garbed. Then came the glass-
workers in scarlet furred with vair, and gold-fringed hoods, and
rich garlands of pearls, carrying flasks and goblets of the famous Venetian glass before them, and the comb and lantern
makers, with a lantern full of birds to let loose in the Doge's
presence, and the goldsmiths wearing wreaths and necklaces
of gold and silver beads and sapphires, emeralds, diamonds,
topazes, jacinths, amethysts, rubies, jasper, and carbuncles.
Masters and servants alike were sumptuously clad, and almost
all wore gold fringes on their hoods and garlands of gilded
beads. Each craft was accompanied by its band of divers instruments, and bore with it silver cups and flagons of wine,
and all marched in fair order, singing ballads and songs of
greeting, and saluted the Doge and Dogaressa in turn, crying
"Long live our lord, the noble Doge Lorenzo Tiepolo!" Gild
after gild they marched in their splendour, lovely alike to
ear and eye; and a week fled before the rejoicings were ended
and all had passed in procession. Canale surpasses himself
here, for he loved State ceremonies; he gives a paragraph to
the advance of each gild, its salutation and withdrawal, and
the cumulative effect of all the paragraphs is enchanting, like
a prose ballade, with a repeated refrain at the end of every
verse.[9]

> What, they lived once thus in Venice, where the merchants
>   were the kings,
> Where St. Mark's is, where the Doges used to wed the sea
>   with rings?

Listening to the magnificent salutation of the Doge by the
priests of St. Mark's, "Criste vince, Criste regne, Criste inpere.
Notre signor Laurens Teuples, Des gracie, inclit Dus de

Venise, Dalmace atque Groace, et dominator de la quarte partie et demi de tot l'enmire de Romanie, sauvement, honor, vie, et victoire. Saint Marc, tu le aie," [10] who, hearing, could have doubted that Venice, defier of Rome and conqueror of Constantinople, was the finest, richest, most beautiful, and most powerful city in the world?

But was she? Listen and judge. Thousands of miles away from Venice, across the lands and seas of Asia, a little south of the Yangtze River and close to the sea stood the city of Kinsai or Hangchow, the capital of the Sung emperors, who ruled Southern China, not yet (in 1268) conquered by the Tartars.[11] Like Venice, Kinsai stood upon lagoons of water and was intersected by innumerable canals. It was a hundred miles in circuit, not counting the suburbs which stretched round it, and there was not a span of ground which was not well peopled. It had twelve great gates, and each of the twelve quarters which lay within the gates was greater than the whole of Venice. Its main street was two hundred feet wide, and ran from end to end of the city, broken every four miles by a great square, lined with houses, gardens, palaces, and the shops of the artisans, who were ruled by its twelve great craft gilds. Parallel with the main street was the chief canal, beside which stood the stone warehouses of the merchants who traded with India. Twelve thousand stone bridges spanned its waterways, and those over the principal canals were high enough to allow ships with their tapering masts to pass below, while the carts and horses passed overhead. In its market-places men chaffered for game and peaches, sea-fish, and wine made of rice and spices; and in the lower part of the surrounding houses were shops, where spices and drugs and silk, pearls and every sort of manufactured article were sold. Up and down the streets of Kinsai moved lords and merchants clad in silk, and the most beautiful ladies in the world swayed languidly past in embroidered litters, with jade pins in their black hair and jewelled earrings swinging against their smooth cheeks.[12]

On one side of this city lay a beautiful lake (famous in Chinese history, and still one of the fairest prospects upon earth), studded with wooded islands, on which stood pavilions with charming names: "Lake Prospect," "Bamboo Chambers," "The House of the Eight Genii," and "Pure Delight." Here, like the Venetians, the men of Kinsai came for pleasure parties in barges, nobly hung and furnished, the cabins painted with flowers and mountain landscapes, and looking out they saw on one side the whole expanse of the city, its palaces, temples, convents, and gardens, and on the other the stretch of clear water, crowded with coloured pleasure boats, over which came echoing the high, clear voices and the tinkling instruments of the revellers. There is no space in which to tell of the King's palace, with its gardens and orchards, its painted pavilions, and the groves where the palace ladies coursed the game with dogs, and, tired of the pastime, flung off their robes and ran to the lake, where they disported themselves like a shoal of silver fishes. But a word must be said of the junks, which came sailing into the harbour four and twenty miles away, and up the river to the city; and of the great concourse of ships which came to Zaiton (perhaps the modern Amoy), the port of the province. Here every year came a hundred times more pepper than came to the whole of Christendom through the Levantine ports. Here from Indo China and the Indies came spices and aloes and sandalwood, nutmegs, spikenard and ebony, and riches beyond mention. Big junks laded these things, together with musk from Tibet, and bales of silk from all the cities of Mansi,* and sailed away in and out of the East India Archipelago, with its spice-laden breezes billowing their sails, to Ceylon. There merchants from Malabar and the great trading cities of Southern India took aboard their cargoes and sold them in turn to Arab merchants, who in their turn sold them to the Venetians in one or other of the Levantine ports. Europeans who saw Zaiton and the other Chinese seaports in after years were wont to say that no one, not even a Venetian, could picture to himself the multitude of

* Mansi or Manji was Southern China and Cathay was Northern China, the boundary between them lying along the River Hoang-Ho on the east and the southern boundary of Shen-si on the west.

trading vessels which sailed upon those Eastern seas and
crowded into those Chinese harbours. They said also with one
accord that Kinsai was without doubt the finest and richest and
noblest city in the world. To the men of Kinsai, Venice would
have been a little suburb and the Levant a backyard. The
whole of the East was their trading field, and their wealth
and civilization were already old when Venice was a handful
of mud huts peopled by fishermen.

Nor was Kinsai alone and unmatched in all its wonder and
beauty, for a three days' journey from it stood Sugui, which to-
day we call Suchow, lying also on the great canal, with its
circumference of twenty miles, its prodigious multitudes
swarming the streets, its physicians, philosophers, and magicians; Sugui, with the ginger which was so common that forty
pounds of it might be bought for the price of a Venetian
silver groat, the silk which was manufactured in such vast
quantities that all the citizens were dressed in it and still
ships laden with it sailed away; Sugui under whose jurisdiction
were sixteen wealthy cities, where trade and the arts flourished.
If you had not seen Hangchow, you would have said that there
was no city in the world, not Venice nor Constantinople nor
another worthy to be named in the same breath with Sugui.
The Chinese indeed, seeing the riches and beauty of these
two cities, doubted whether even the pleasant courts of heaven
could show their equal and proudly quoted the proverb:

> *Shang yeu t'ien t'ang,*
> *Hia yeu Su Hang.*

> (There's Paradise above, 'tis true,
> But here below we've Hang and Su.) [13]

Kinsai seems far enough away in all conscience from Venice
in the year 1268, and Venice was all unwitting of its existence,
far beyond the sunrise. Yet there was in the city of the lagoons
that year, watching the same procession of the gilds which
Canale watched, a boy who was destined to link them for ever
in the minds of men—a lean lad of fourteen, Marco Polo by
name, who was always kicking his heels on the quay and bother-

ing foreign sailors for tales of distant lands. He heard all they had to tell him very willingly, storing it up in that active brain of his, for his curiosity was insatiable; but always the tales that he heard most willingly were about the Tartars.

At this time the Tartars were at the height of their power in the West and the East. Tartars ruled at Peking all over Northern China, Corea, Mongolia, Manchuria, and Tibet, and took tribute from Indo China and Java. Tartars were spread over Central Asia, holding sway in Turkestan and Afghanistan. The Golden Horde ruled the Caucasus, a large part of Russia, and a piece of Siberia. Tartars held sway in Persia, Georgia, Armenia, and a part of Asia Minor. When the great Mangu Khan died in 1259, one empire lay spread across Asia and Europe, from the Yellow River to the Danube. There had been nothing like it in the world before, and there was nothing like it again, until the Russian Empire of modern times. By 1268 it was beginning to split up into the four kingdoms of China, Central Asia, Russia, and Persia, but still it was one people. Now, the attitude of the West to the Tartars at this time was very interesting. At first it feared them as a new scourge of God, like Attila and his Huns; they overran Poland, ravaged Hungary, and seemed about to break like a great flood upon the West, and overwhelm it utterly. Then the tide rolled back. Gradually the West lost its first stupefaction and terror and began to look hopefully towards the Tartars as a possible ally against its age-old foe, the Moslem. The Christians of the West knew that the Tartars had laid the Moslem power low through the length and breadth of Asia, and they knew too, that the Tartars had no very sharply defined faith and were curious of all beliefs that came their way. Gradually the West became convinced that the Tartars might be converted to Christianity, and fight side by side beneath the Cross against the hated Crescent. There grew up the strange legend of Prester John, a Christian priest-king, ruling somewhere in the heart of Asia; and indeed little groups of Nestorian Christians did still survive in Eastern Asia at this time.[14] Embassies began to pass between Tartar khans and Western monarchs, and there began also a great series of missions of Franciscan friars to Tartary, men who were ethnologists and geographers at heart as well as missionaries, and have left us priceless accounts of the lands which they visited. In the year of grace 1268, much was known about Central Asia, for in 1245 the Pope had sent the Italian friar John of Plano Carpini thither, and in 1251 another friar, William of Rubruck, a French Fleming, had been sent by the saintly Louis, King of France. Both got as far as Karakorum, the Tartar camp on the borders of Northern China, though they did not enter China itself. They had brought back innumerable stories about the nomad conquerors, who carried their tents on carts, and drank fermented mares' milk, about the greatness of the khan and his welcome to the strangers from the West, and the interest with which he listened to their preaching.[15] These tales were common property now, and Marco Polo must have listened to them.

Marco Polo was always talking of the Tartars, always asking about them. Indeed, he had reason to be interested in them. This (as we have said) was the year of grace 1268, and eight years before (some, indeed, say fifteen years) his father, Nicolo Polo, and his uncle Maffeo had vanished into Tartary. They were rich merchants, trading with their own ship to Constantinople, and there they had decided to go on a commercial venture into the lands of the Golden Horde, which lay to the north of the Black Sea. So they had sailed over to the Crimea, where they had a counting-house at Soldaia, and taking with them a store of costly jewels, for they were jewel merchants, they had set off on horseback to visit the Khan of the West Tartars. So much the Venetians knew, for word had come back from Soldaia of their venture; but they had never returned. And so Marco, kicking his heels upon the quay, caught sailor-men by the sleeve and asked them about those wild horsemen with their mares' milk and their magicians and their droves of cattle; and as he asked he wondered about his father and his uncle, and whether they were dead and lost for ever in the wilds of Tartary. But even while he asked and wondered and kicked his heels on the quay, while the Doge Tiepolo was watching the procession of the gilds and the clerk Canale was adding up customs dues or writing the ancient history of

the Venetians, at that very moment the two Polos were slowly
and wearily making their way across the heights of Central
Asia with a caravan of mules and camels, drawing near to
golden Samarcand with its teeming bazaars, coming nearer
and nearer to the West; and in the following year, 1269, they
reached Acre, and took ship there for Venice, and so at last
came home.

They had a strange story to tell, stranger and better than
anything the lean, inquisitive boy had heard upon the quays.
They had soon disposed of their jewels and they had spent a
year at the camp of the Khan of the Golden Horde of Kipchak
on the mighty River Volga. Then war broke out between that
ruler and the Khan who ruled the Persian Khanate, and it cut
off their way back. But Marco's curiosity was inherited; and no
Venetian was ever averse to seeing strange lands and seeking
out new opportunities for trade; so the Polos decided to go on
and visit the Khan of Central Asia or Chagatai, and perhaps
make their way back to Constantinople by some unfrequented
route. They struggled over plains peopled only by tent-dwell-
ing Tartars and their herds, until at last they reached the noble
city of Bokhara. They must have followed the line of the
Oxus River, and if we reverse the marvellous description which
Matthew Arnold wrote of that river's course in *Sohrad and
Rustum*, we shall have a picture of the Polos' journey:

> But the majestic River floated on,
> Out of the mist and hum of that low land,
> Into the frosty starlight, and there moved,
> Rejoicing, through the hush'd Chorasmian waste
> Under the solitary moon; he flow'd
> Right for the Polar Star, past Orgunjè,
> Brimming and bright and large: then sands begin
> To hem his watery march, and dam his streams,
> And split his currents; that for many a league
> The shorn and parcell'd Oxus strains along
> Through beds of sand and matted rushy isles—
> Oxus, forgetting the bright speed he had
> In his high mountain cradle in Pamere,

A foil'd circuitous wanderer:—till at last
The long'd-for dash of waves is heard, and wide
His luminous home of waters opens, bright
And tranquil, from whose floor the new-bathed stars
Emerge and shine upon the Aral Sea.

For three years the Polos remained at Bokhara, until one day it happened that an embassy came to the city, on its way back from the khan in Persia to the great Khan Kublai, who ruled in far-off China, and to whom all the Tartar rulers owed allegiance. The chief ambassador was struck with the talents and charm of the brothers, who had now become proficient in the Tartar language, and persuaded them to accompany him on his journey to the presence of the Great Khan, who had never yet set eyes on a man of the West, and would, he assured them, receive them honourably. They would not have been Venetians had they refused such an opportunity, and, taking their Venetian servants with them, they journeyed for a year with the Tartar embassy across the heart of Asia, and so reached the great Kublai Khan. Many years later Marco himself described their reception, as they had told it to him:

Being introduced to the presence of the Grand Khan Kublai, the travellers were received by him with the condescension and affability that belonged to his character, and as they were the first Latins who had made their appearance in that country, they were entertained with feasts and honoured with other marks of distinction. Entering graciously into conversation with them, he made earnest inquiries on the subject of the western parts of the world, of the Emperor of the Romans, and of other christian kings and princes . . . and above all he questioned them particularly respecting the Pope, the affairs of the Church, and the religious worship and doctrine of the Christians. Being well instructed and discreet men, they gave appropriate answers upon all these points, and as they were perfectly acquainted with the Tartar language, they expressed themselves always in becoming terms; insomuch that the Grand Khan, holding them in high estimation, frequently commanded their attendance.[16]

The Great Khan finally decided to send these two intelligent strangers back to their own land on a mission from himself to the Pope, asking for a hundred men of learning to be sent to teach and preach to his Tartars, and for some holy oil from the lamp which burned over Christ's sepulchre in Jerusalem. He provided them with a golden tablet of honour, which acted as a passport and secured that they should be entertained and their journey facilitated from city to city in all his dominions, and so they set forth once more upon their homeward journey. But they were delayed by the dangers and difficulties of travel, "the extreme cold, the snow, the ice, and the flooding of the rivers," and it was three years before they at last reached Acre in the April of 1269, and finding that the Pope had died the year before, and that no election had yet been made, so that they could not immediately accomplish their mission, they decided to visit their home again, and so went back to Venice. There Nicolo found that his wife, who had been with child at his departure, was dead, leaving behind her a son Marco, our young haunter of quays.

This was the marvellous tale which the same Marco drank in from the lips of his new-found father and uncle. But more marvels were to come. For two years the Venetians remained at home, awaiting the election of a Pope in order to deliver the Great Khan's letters; but no election was made, and at last, fearing that Kublai might suspect them of playing him false, they decided to return to the East, and this time they took with them Marco, now a well-grown lad of sixteen or seventeen years with a bright eye that looked everywhere and took in everything, observant and sober beyond his age. But when they got as far as Ayas on the Gulf of Scanderoon, news was brought them of the election of Tebaldo di Piacenza as Pope Gregory X, and as Tebaldo had already interested himself in their mission, they returned with all speed to Acre, and obtained from him letters to the Khan (they had already visited Jerusalem and provided themselves with some of the holy oil), and two Dominican friars, "men of letters and science as well as profound theologians," though not the hundred men of learning for whom the Khan had asked; and so they set out again from Acre in November, 1271. The Dominicans may have been profound theologians, but they were somewhat chicken-hearted adventurers, and when rumours reached them of wars in the district of Armenia, through which they had to pass, they hastily handed over their letters to the Venetians, put themselves under the protection of the Knights Templars, and scuttled back to the coast and safety as fast as they could go, leaving the Polos, "undismayed by perils and difficulties, to which they had long been inured," to proceed alone. Assuredly, St. Francis crows over St. Dominic somewhere in the courts of Heaven; his friars never feared for their skins, as they travelled blithely into the heat of India and the cold of Central Asia; and it is easy to imagine the comments of fat William of Rubruck upon the flight of the profound theologians.

The account of this second journey of the Polos may be read in the wonderful book which Marco afterwards wrote to describe the wonders of the world. They went from Lajazzo through Turcomania, past Mount Ararat, where Marco heard tell that Noah's ark rested, and where he first heard also of the oil wells of Baku and the great inland sea of Caspain. Past Mosul and Bagdad they went through Persia, where brocades are woven and merchants bring caravan after caravan of treasures, to Hormuz, on the Persian Gulf, into which port put the ships from India, laden with spices, drugs, scented woods, and jewels, gold tissues and elephants' teeth. Here they meant to take ship, but they desisted, perhaps because they feared to trust themselves to the flimsy nailless vessels in which the Arabs braved the dangers of the Indian Ocean. So they turned north again and prepared to make the journey by land. They traversed the salt desert of Kerman, through Balk and Khorassan to Badakhshan, where there are horses bred from Alexander the Great's steed Bucephalus, and ruby mines and lapis lazuli. It is a land of beautiful mountains and wide plains, of trout streams and good hunting, and here the brothers sojourned for nearly a year, for young Marco had fallen ill in the hot plains: a breath of mountain air blows through the page in which he describes how amid the clean winds his health

came back to him. When he was well, they went on again, and
ascended the upper Oxus to the highlands of Pamir, "the roof
of the world" as it has been called in our own time, a land of
icy cold, where Marco saw and described the great horned
sheep which hunters and naturalists still call after him the
Ovis Poli,[17] a land which no traveller (save Benedict Goës,
about 1604) described again, until Lieutenant John Wood of
the Indian Navy went there in 1838. Thence they descended
upon Kashgar, Yarkand, and Khotan, where jade is found,
regions which no one visited again until 1860. From Khotan
they pushed on to the vicinity of Lake Lob, never to be reached
again until a Russian explorer got there in 1871. They halted
there to load asses and camels with provisions, and then,
with sinking hearts, they began the terrible thirty days' journey
across the Gobi Desert. Marco gives a vivid description of its
terrors, voices which seem to call the traveller by name, the
march of phantom cavalcades, which lures them off the road at
night, spirits which fill the air with sounds of music, drums and
gongs and the clash of arms—all those illusions which human
beings have heard and seen and feared in every desert and in
every age.

> What might this be? A thousand fantasies
> Begin to throng into my memory,
> Of calling shapes, and beckoning shadows dire,
> And airy tongues that syllable men's names
> On sands and shores and desert wildernesses.

At last they arrived safely at Tangut in the extreme north-
west of China, and, skirting the frontier across the great
steppes of Mongolia, they were greeted by the Khan's people,
who had been sent forward to meet them at the distance of
forty days' journey, and so at last they reached his presence in
the May of 1275, having journeyed for three years and a half.

The Great Khan received the Polos kindly, listened atten-
tively to the account which they gave of their mission, commended them for their zeal and fidelity, and received the holy
oil and the Pope's gifts with reverence. He then observed the
boy Marco, now a "young gallant" and personable enough, no

doubt, and inquired who he was, and Nicolo made answer,
"Sire, this is your servant, and my son," to which the Khan
replied, "He is welcome, and much it pleases me," and enrolled Marco among his own attendants. It was the beginning
of a long and close association, for Kublai Khan soon found
that Marco Polo was both discreet and intelligent, and began
to employ him on various missions. Moreover, Marco, for his
part, found that the Great Khan was always desirous of learning the manners and customs of the many tribes over whom he
ruled. Kublai had to the full that noble curiosity which is the
beginning of wisdom, and it irked him exceedingly that his
envoys, good conscientious men, followed their noses upon
his business, looking neither to right nor to left, and as like as
not never even noticed that among the aboriginal hill tribes of
the interior called Miaotzu there prevailed the peculiar and
entertaining custom of the *couvade*, wherein

> Chineses go to bed
> And lie in, in their ladies' stead.[18]

"The Prince, in consequence," says Marco, "held them for no
better than fools and dolts and would say, 'I had far liever
hearken about the strange things and the manners of the different countries you have seen than merely be told of the business you went upon.'"

Very different was the habit of the Venetian, who as a lad
had lent ear so readily to swarthy sailors on the Rialto. He
quickly picked up several of the languages current in the Great
Khan's empire, and here is his account of his proceedings when
on a mission to foreign parts:

Perceiving that the Great Khan took a pleasure in hearing
accounts of whatever was new to him respecting the customs
and manners of people, and the peculiar circumstances of distant countries, he endeavoured, wherever he went, to obtain
correct information on these subjects and made notes of all he
saw and heard, in order to gratify the curiosity of his master.
In short, during seventeen years that he continued in his service, he rendered himself so useful, that he was employed on

confidential missions to every part of the empire and its dependencies; and sometimes also he travelled on his own private account, but always with the consent and sanctioned by the authority of the Grand Khan. In such circumstances it was that Marco Polo had the opportunity of acquiring a knowledge, either by his own observation or by what he collected from others, of so many things until his time unknown, respecting the Eastern parts of the world, and these he diligently and regularly committed to writing. . . . And by this means he obtained so much honour that he provoked the jealousy of other officers of the court.[19]

It is small wonder that when first the lad came back with his reports the Great Khan and his courtiers marvelled and exclaimed, "If this young man live he will assuredly be a person of great worth and ability."

It was while on these various public missions that Marco Polo journeyed through the provinces of Shansi, Shensi, and Szechuen, and skirted the edge of Tibet to Yunnan, and entered Northern Burma, lands unknown again to the West until after 1860. For three years he was himself governor of the great city of Yangchow, which had twenty-four towns under its jurisdiction, and was full of traders and makers of arms and military accoutrements.[20] He visited Karakorum in Mongolia, the old Tartar capital, and with his Uncle Maffeo spent three years in Tangut. On another occasion he went on a mission to Cochin China, and by sea to the southern states of India, and he has left a vivid picture of the great trading cities of Malabar. He might indeed have pondered with Ulysses,

> I am become a name
> For always roaming with a hungry heart,
> Much have I seen and known, cities of men,
> And manners, climates, countries, governments,
> Myself not least, but honoured of them all.

He describes the great capital Cambaluc (Peking) in the north, and the beautiful Kinsai (Hangchow) in the south. He describes the Khan's summer palace at Shandu, with its woods and gardens, its marble palace, its bamboo pavilion swung like a tent from two hundred silken cords, its stud of white mares, and its wonder-working magicians. Indeed his description of the summer palace is better known to Englishmen than any other part of his work, for Shandu is Xanadu, which Coleridge saw in a dream after he had been reading Marco's book and wove into wonderful verse:

> In Xanadu did Kubla Khan
> A stately pleasure dome decree,
> Where Alph the sacred river ran,
> Through caverns measureless to man,
> Down to a sunless sea.

> And there were gardens bright with sinuous rills
> Where blossomed many an incense bearing tree,
> And here were forests, ancient as the hills
> Enfolding sunny spots of greenery.

Nor is it only palaces which Marco Polo describes, for he tells of the great canal and inland river trade of China, the exports and imports at its harbours, the paper money, the system of posts and caravanserais, which linked it together. He gives an unsurpassed picture of that huge, rich, peaceful empire, full of wealth and commerce and learned men and beautiful things, and of its ruler Kublai Khan, one of the noblest monarchs who ever sat upon a throne, who, since "China is a sea that salts all the rivers that flow into it," [21] was far more than a barbarous Mongol khan, was in very truth a Chinese emperor, whose house, called by the Chinese the "Yuan Dynasty," takes its place among the great dynasties of China.

Even more than Marco Polo tells us he must, indeed, have seen. The impersonality of the greater part of the book is its one blemish, for we would fain know more of how he lived in China. There is some evidence that he consorted with the Mongol conquerors rather than with the Chinese, and that Chinese was not one of the languages which he learned. He makes no mention of several characteristic Chinese customs, such as the compressed feet of the women, and fishing with

cormorants (both of which are described by Odoric of Pordenone after him); he travelled through the tea districts of
Fo-kien, but he never mentions tea-drinking, and he has no
word to say even of the Great Wall.[22] And how typical a
European he is, in some ways, for all his keen interest in
new and strange things. "They are," he says of the peaceful
merchants and scholars of Suchow, "a pusillanimous race and
solely occupied with their trade and manufactures. In these
indeed they display considerable ability, and if they were as
enterprising, manly, and warlike as they are ingenious, so prodigious is their number that they might not only subdue the
whole of the province, but carry their rule further still." [23]
Nearly five hundred years later we find the same judgment
expressed in different words: "Better fifty years of Europe than
a cycle of Cathay." The answer is a question: Would you
rather be the pusillanimous Chinese, who painted the landscape roll of which a portion is reproduced [in the original
edition], or the enterprising, manly, and warlike European of
the same period, whose highest achievement in pictorial art is
the picture of Marco Polo's embarkation [also reproduced
there]? What is civilization and what progress? Yet Marco Polo
shows himself throughout his book far from unable to appreci-
ate other standards than those of his own land and religion,
for of Sakya-muni Buddha he says that, "had he been a Christian he would have been a great saint of our Lord Jesus Christ,"
and he could honour Kublai as that great Khan deserved.

Nevertheless, although Marco Polo shows less knowledge
of the Chinese than one might expect from the extraordinary
detail and fidelity of his observation in other directions, he
must have known many of these charming and cultivated
people, at Kinsai or Cambaluc, or at the city which he governed. Among others, he must have known the great artist who
painted the roll mentioned above, Chao Mêng-fu, whom the
Chinese called "*Sung hsüeh Tao jen,*" or the "Apostle of Pine
Trees and Snow." He was a lineal descendant of the founder
of the Sung dynasty and a hereditary official. When that
dynasty at last fell before the Tartars, he and his friend Ch'ien
Hsüan, "the Man of the Jade Pool and Roaring Torrent,"

retired into private life. But in 1286 Chao Mêng-fu was summoned to court by Kublai Khan, and, to the indignation of
his friend, returned and became secretary in the Board of War,
occupying his time in this post (what must Marco Polo have
thought of him!) in painting his marvellous pictures. He became a great favourite of the Khan and was always about the
court, and Marco Polo must have known him well and perhaps have watched him at work painting those matchless landscapes, and those pictures of horses and men for which he was
famous. Marco loved horses, as, indeed, he loved all kinds of
sport (of which he had plenty, for the Khan was a great hunter
and hawker), and he has left a word picture of the white brood
mares at Shansi, which may be set beside Chao Mêng-fu's
brush picture of the "Eight Horses in the Park of Kublai
Khan." [24] He knew, too, perhaps Chao Mêng-fu's wife, the
Lady Kuan, who painted most exquisitely the graceful bamboo and the peony, so loved by Chinese artists, and of whom it
is related that "she would watch the moving shadows of the
sprays thrown by the moon on the paper windows, and trans-
fer the fugitive outlines to paper with a few strokes of her
supple brush, so that every smallest scrap of her work was
mounted in albums as models for others to copy." [25] Chao
Mêng-fu and the Lady Kuan had a son, Chao Yung, who is of
special interest to us, for he painted a picture of a Tangut
hunter, and Marco Polo has also given a description of the
Tartar horsemen and of the province of Tangut, where he
saw and described the musk deer and the yak.

But we must return to the history of the Polos in China.
From time to time in Marco's book we hear also of his father
and uncle, travelling about the empire, growing rich by trade,
and amassing a store of those jewels, in the value of which
they were so skilled, even helping the Khan to reduce a rebel
town, by constructing siege engines for him on the European
model, handy Venetians that they were, who could lay their
hands to anything.[27] Without doubt they were proud of their
Marco, who from an inquisitive lad had grown to so wise and
observant a man, and had risen to so high a position. So for
seventeen years the three Polos abode in the Khan's service in

China. The long months slipped by; and at last they began to
feel upon them a longing to see Venice and the lagoons again,
and to hear Mass once more beneath the majestic roof of St.
Mark's before they died. Moreover, Kublai Khan was growing old himself, and the favour which he had always shown
to them had excited some jealousy among his own people,
and they feared what might happen when he died. But the
old Khan was adamant to all their prayers; wealth and honours
were theirs for the asking, but he would not let them go. They
might, indeed, have died in China, and we of the West might
never have heard of Marco Polo or of Kublai Khan, but for a
mere accident, a stroke of fate, which gave them their chance.
In 1286 Arghun, the Khan of Persia, lost by death his favourite wife Bolgana, and, according to her dying wish, he sent
ambassadors to the Court of Peking to ask for another bride
from her own Mongol tribe. Their overland route home again
was endangered by a war, and they therefore proposed to return by sea. Just at that moment, Marco Polo happened to
return from a voyage on which he had been sent, and spoke
with such assurance of the ease with which it had been accomplished, that the three ambassadors conceived a strong desire
to take with them all three of these ingenious Venetians, who
seemed to know so much about ships. Thus it was that the
great Khan was prevailed upon, very reluctantly, to let them
go.

Early in 1292 they set sail from the busy port of Zaiton in
fourteen big Chinese junks (of which Marco, writing of the
shipping of the Indian and China seas, has left an excellent
description),[28] with the three envoys, the princess, a beautiful
girl of seventeen, "moult bele dame at avenant," says Marco,
who had an eye for pretty ladies, and a large suite of attendants. One version of Marco's book says that they took with
them also the daughter of the king of Mansi, one of those
Sung princesses who in happier days had wandered beside the
lake in Hangchow, and who had no doubt been brought up at
Cambaluc by the care of Kublai Khan's favourite queen, the
Lady Jamui. The voyage was a long and difficult one; they suffered lengthy delays in Sumatra, Ceylon, and Southern India,

occupied by Marco in studying the sea charts of the coast of India which the Arab pilots showed him, and adding to his knowledge of these parts, which he had already visited. Thus it was over two years before the junks reached Persia, and two of the three envoys and a large number of their suite had died by the way. When at last they landed, it was found that Arghun, the prospective bridegroom, had meanwhile died too, leaving his throne in the charge of a regent for his young son. But on the regent's advice a convenient solution of the difficulty was found by handing the princess over to this prince, and Marco and his uncles duly conducted her to him in the province of Timochain, where Marco Polo noticed that the women were "in my opinion the most beautiful in the world," where stood the famed and solitary *arbor secco*, and where men still told tales of great Alexander and Darius. There they took leave of their princess, who had come on the long voyage to love them like fathers, so Marco says, and wept sorely when they parted. It was while they were still in Persia, where they stayed for nine months after handing over the princess, that the Polos received news of the death of the Great Khan whom they had served so faithfully for so many years. He died at the ripe age of eighty, and with his death a shadow fell over the Central Asia, darkening the shining yellow roofs of Cambaluc,

> the barren plains
> Of Sericana, where Chinese drive
> With sails and wind their cany waggons light,

the minarets of Persia, and the tents of wild Kipchak Tartars, galloping over the Russian steppes. So wide had been the sway of Kublai Khan. A shadow fell also upon the heart of Marco Polo. It was as though a door had clanged to behind him, never to open again. "In the course of their journey," he says, "our travellers received intelligence of the Great Khan having departed this life, which entirely put an end to all prospects of their revisiting those regions." So he and his elders went on by way of Tabriz, Trebizond, and Constantinople to Venice, and sailed up to the city of the lagoons at long last at the end of 1295.

A strange fairy-tale legend has come down to us about the return of the Polos. "When they got thither," says Ramusio, who edited Marco's book in the fifteenth century, "the same fate befell them as befell Ulysses, who when he returned after his twenty years' wanderings to his native Ithaca was recognized by nobody." When, clad in their uncouth Tartar garb, the three Polos knocked at the doors of the Ca' Polo, no one recognized them, and they had the greatest difficulty in persuading their relatives and fellow-Venetians that they were indeed those Polos who had been believed dead for so many years. The story goes that they satisfactorily established their identity by inviting all their kinsmen to a great banquet, for each course of which they put on a garment more magnificent than the last, and finally, bringing in their coarse Tartar coats, they ripped open the seams and the lining thereof, "upon which there poured forth a great quantity of precious stones, rubies, sapphires, carbuncles, diamonds, and emeralds, which had been sewn into each coat with great care, so that nobody could have suspected that anything was there. . . . The exhibition of such an extraordinary and infinite treasure of jewels and precious stones, which covered the table, once more filled all present with such astonishment that they were dumb and almost beside themselves with surprise: and they at once recognized these honoured and venerated gentlemen in the Ca' Polo, whom at first they had doubted, and received them with the greatest honour and reverence." [29] Human nature has changed little since the thirteenth century. The precious stones are a legend, but no doubt the Polos brought many with them, for they were jewel merchants by trade; they had had ample opportunities for business in China, and the Great Khan had loaded them with "rubies and other handsome jewels of great value" to boot. Jewels were the most convenient form in which they could have brought home their wealth. But the inquiring Marco brought other things also to tickle the curiosity of the Venetians, as he lets fall from time to time in his book. He brought, for example, specimens of the silky hair of the Tangut yak, which his countrymen much admired, the dried head and feet of a musk deer, and the seeds of a dye plant (probably indigo) from Sumatra, which he sowed in Venice, but which never came up, because the climate was not sufficiently warm.[30] He brought presents also for the Doge; for an inventory made in 1351 of things found in the palace of Marino Faliero includes among others a ring given by Kublai Khan, a Tartar collar, a three-bladed sword, an Indian brocade, and a book "written by the hand of the aforesaid Marco," called *De locis mirabilibus Tartarorum.*[31]

The rest of Marco Polo's life is quickly told. The legend goes that all the youth of Venice used to resort to the Ca' Polo in order to hear his stories, for not even among the foreign sailors on the quays, where once the boy Marco had wandered and asked about the Tartars, were stories the like of his to be heard. And because he was always talking of the greatness of Kublai Khan's dominions, the millions of revenue, the millions of junks, the millions of riders, the millions of towns and cities, they gave him a nickname and jestingly called him Marco *Milione,* or *Il Milione,* which is, being interpreted, "Million Marco"; and the name even crept into the public documents of the Republic, while the courtyard of his house became known as the *Corte Milione.* To return from legend to history, the ancient rivalry between Venice and Genoa had been growing during Marco Polo's absence, nor had Venice always prevailed. Often as her galleys sailed,

> dipping deep
> For Famagusta and the hidden sun
> That rings black Cyprus with a lake of fire, . . .
> Questing brown slaves or Syrian oranges,
> The pirate Genoese
> Hell raked them till they rolled
> Blood, water, fruit, and corpses up the hold.

At last in 1298, three years after Marco's return, a Genoese fleet under Lamba Doria sailed for the Adriatic, to bate the pride of Venice in her own sea. The Venetians fitted out a great fleet to meet it, and Marco Polo, the handy man who knew so much about navigation, albeit more skilled with Chinese junks than with Western ships, went with it as gentleman commander of a galley. The result of the encounter was a shattering victory for the Genoese off Curzola. Sixty-eight Venetian galleys were burnt, and seven thousand prisoners were haled off to Genoa, among them Marco Polo, who had now a taste of the results of that enterprise, manliness, and warfare, whose absence he so deprecated in the men of Suchow.

But soon there began to run through the streets and courtyards of Genoa a rumour that in prison there lay a certain Venetian captain, with tales so wonderful to beguile the passing hour that none could tire of hearing them; and anon the gallants and sages and the bold ladies of Genoa were flocking, just as the men of the Rialto had flocked before, to hear his stories of Kublai Khan,

> Lord of the fruits of Tartary
>   Her rivers silver-pale,
> Lord of the hills of Tartary,
>   Glen, thicket, wood, and dale,
> Her flashing stars, her scented breeze,
> Her trembling lakes, like foamless seas,
> Her bird-delighting citron-trees
>   In every purple vale.

"Messer Marco," so runs Ramusio's account of the tradition which lingered in Venice in his day, "finding himself in this position, and witnessing the general eagerness to hear all about Cathay and the Great Khan, which indeed compelled him daily to repeat his story till he was weary, was advised to put the matter in writing, so he found means to get a letter written to his father in Venice, in which he desired the latter to send those notes and memoranda, which he had brought home with him."

It happened that in prison with Marco Polo there lay a certain Pisan writer of romances, Rusticiano by name,[32] who had probably been taken prisoner before at the battle of Melaria (1284), when so many Pisan captives had been carried to Genoa, that the saying arose "He who would see Pisa let him go to Genoa." Rusticiano was skilled in the writing of French, the language *par excellence* of romances, in which he had written versions of the Round Table Tales, and in him Marco Polo found a ready scribe, who took down the stories as he told them, in the midst of the crowd of Venetian prisoners and Genoese gentlemen, raptly drinking in all the wonders of Kublai Khan. It was by a just instinct that, when all was written, Rusticiano prefixed to the tale that same address to the lords and gentlemen of the world, bidding them to take heed and listen, which he had been wont to set at the beginning of his tales of Tristan and Lancelot and King Arthur: "Ye Lords, Emperors and Kings, Dukes and Marquises, Counts, Knights and Burgesses and all ye men who desire to know the divers races of men and the diversities of the different regions of the world, take ye this book and cause it to be read, and here shall ye find the greatest marvels." But he adds, "Marco Polo, a wise and learned citizen of Venice, states distinctly what things he saw and what things he heard from others, for this book will be a truthful one." Marco Polo's truthful marvels were more wonderful even than the exploits of Arthur's knights, and were possibly better suited to the respectable Rusticiano's pen, for his only other claim to distinction in the eyes of posterity seems to be that in his abridgement of the Romance of Lancelot he entirely omits the episode (if episode it can be called) of the loves of Lancelot and Guinevere. "Alas," remarks his French editor, "that copy of Lancelot which fell into the hands of poor Francesca of Rimini was not one of those expurgated by Rusticiano!" [33]

Marco Polo was released from prison (there must have been mourning in the palaces of Genoa) and returned to Venice at the end of a year. Sometimes hereafter his name occurs in the records of Venice, as he moves about on his lawful occasions.[34] In 1305 we find "Nobilis Marchus Polo Milioni" standing surety for a wine smuggler; in 1311 he is suing a dishonest agent who owes him money on the sale of musk (he, Marco, had seen the musk deer in its lair); and in 1323 he is concerned in a dispute about a party wall. We know too, from his will, that he had a wife named Donata, and three daughters, Fantina, Bellela, and Moreta. Had he loved before, under the alien skies where his youth was spent, some languid, exquisite

lady of China, or hardy Tartar maid? Had he profited himself
from the strange marriage customs of Tibet, of which he remarks (with one of his very rare gleams of humour), "En
cele contree aurent bien aler les jeune de seize anz en vingt
quatre"? Had Fantina, Bellela, and Moreta half-brothers, fly-
ing their gerfalcons at the quails by the shores of the "White
Lake" where the Khan hunted, and telling tales of the half
legendary father, who sailed away for ever when they were
boys in the days of Kublai Khan? These things we cannot
know, nor can we even guess whether he regretted that only
daughters sprang from his loins in the city of the lagoons, and
no Venetian son to go venturing again to the far-distant country where assuredly he had left a good half of his heart. Perhaps he talked of it sometimes to Peter, his Tartar servant,
whom he freed at his death "from all bondage as completely as
I pray God to release mine own soul from all sin and guilt."
Some have thought that he brought Peter the Tartar with him
from the East, and the thought is a pleasant one; but it is
more likely that he bought him in Italy, for the Venetians
were inveterate slave-owners, and captive Tartars were held of
all the slaves the strongest and best. So his life passed; and in
1324 Marco Polo died, honoured much by his fellow-citizens,
after making a will which is still preserved in the library of
St. Mark's.

A characteristic story of his death-bed is related by a
Dominican friar, one Jacopo of Acqui, who wrote some time
later. "What he told in the book," says Jacopo, "was not as
much as he had really seen, because of the tongues of de-
tractors, who being ready to impose their own lies on others
are over hasty to set down as lies what they in their perversity
disbelieve or do not understand. And because there are many
great and strange things in that book, which are reckoned
past all credence, he was asked by his friends on his death-
bed to correct the book, by removing everything that went
beyond the facts. To which his reply was that he had not
told *one half* of what he had really seen." [35] How well one
can see that last indignant flash of the dying observer, who
in the long years of his youth had taken notes of strange

tribes and customs for the wise and gracious Kublai Khan, and whom little men now dared to doubt. Indeed, modern discovery has entirely confirmed the exactitude of Marco Polo's observation. It is true that he sometimes repeated some very tall stories which had been told to him, of dog-faced men in the Andaman Islands and of the "male and female islands" so beloved of medieval geographers. These were sailors' yarns, and where Marco Polo reports what he has seen with his own eyes, he reports with complete accuracy, nor does he ever pretend to have seen a place which he had not visited. The explorers of our own day, Aurel Stein, Ellsworth Huntington, and Sven Hedin, travelling in Central Asia, have triumphantly vindicated him. "It is," says an eminent French historian, "as though the originals of very old photographs had been suddenly rediscovered: the old descriptions of things which were unchanged could be perfectly superimposed upon present reality," [36] and Huntington and Aurel Stein took with them to the inaccessible districts of Central Asia as guidebooks the book of the Chinese pilgrim Hiwen Thsang (seventh century) and the book of Marco Polo, and over and over again found how accurate were their descriptions.

It is indeed almost impossible to exaggerate the extent of Marco Polo's accomplishment. It is best estimated in the often-quoted words of Sir Henry Yule, whose edition of his book is one of the great works of English scholarship:

He was the first traveller to trace a route across the whole longitude of Asia, naming and describing kingdom after kingdom, which he had seen with his own eyes, the desert of Persia, the flowering plateaux and wild gorges of Badakhshan, the jade-bearing rivers of Khotan, the Mongol steppes, cradle of the power that had so lately threatened to swallow up Christendom, the new and brilliant court that had been established at Cambaluc: the first Travellers to reveal China in all its wealth and vastness, its mighty rivers, its huge cities, its rich manufactures, its swarming population, the inconceivably vast fleets that quickened its seas and inland waters; to tell us of the nations on its borders with all their eccen-

Extent of Tartar domin-
ions in Marco Polo's day.
First journey of the two
elder Polos.
Outward route of Marco Polo
& some of his journeys
in China.
Homeward route of Marco Polo

tricities of manners and worship; of Tibet and its sordid devo-
tees; of Burma with its golden pagodas and their tinkling
crowns; of Laos, of Siam, of Cochin China, of Japan, the

A Map of the
JOURNEYS
of the
POLOS

Karakorum

Shengtu

MONGOLIA

GOBI DESERT

TANGUT

GREAT WALL

Cambaluc

CATHAY

EMPIRE of the

Yangui Shgui

Kinsai

TIBET

MANZI

Zaiton

SUMATRA

BORNEO

Eastern Thule, with its rosy pearls and golden-roofed palaces;
the first to speak of that Museum of Beauty and Wonder,
still so imperfectly ransacked, the Indian Archipelago, source

of those aromatics then so highly prized and whose origin
was so dark; of Java the Pearl of Islands; of Sumatra with its
many kings, its strange costly products, and its cannibal races;
of the naked savages of Nicobar and Andaman; of Ceylon,
the Isle of Gems, with its Sacred Mountain and its Tomb of
Adam; of India the Great, not as a dreamland of Alexandrian
fables, but as a country seen and partially explored, with its
virtuous Brahmans, its obscene ascetics, its diamonds and the
strange tales of their acquisition, its sea-beds of pearl and its
powerful sun; the first in modern times to give any distinct
account of the secluded Christian Empire of Abyssinia, to
speak, though indeed dimly, of Zanzibar with its negroes and
its ivory and of the vast and distant Madagascar, bordering
on the Dark Ocean of the South, with its Ruc and other
monstrosities; and in a remotely opposite region, of Siberia
and the Arctic Ocean, of dogsledges, white bears and rein-
deer-riding Tunguses.[37]

The knowledge which Marco Polo had thus brought to
Europe, the intercourse between East and West which his
experience had shown to be so desirable, continued to grow
after him. Merchants and missionaries alike travelled by land
or sea eastward to Cathay.[38] Another of those indomitable
Franciscan friars, John of Monte Corvino, went out at the
age of fifty and became Archbishop of Peking. Churches and
houses of friars were founded in some of the Chinese cities.
Odoric of Pordenone, another friar, and a very good observer
too, set forth in 1316 and sailed round India and through the
Spice Islands by the same sea route by which the Polos had
brought their Tartar princess back to Persia, and so reached
Canton, "a city as big as three Venices . . . and all Italy hath
not the amount of craft that this one city hath." He left a
wonderful account of his travels in China, including descriptions of Peking and Hangchow, and ends his stories with the
words, "As for me, from day to day I prepare myself to return
to those countries, in which I am content to die, if it pleaseth
Him from whom all good things do come"—no doubt where
he had left his heart, but he died at Udine in Italy. Later

there went out another friar, John Marignolli, who was Papal
Legate to Peking from 1342 to 1346.

Nor was it only missionaries who went to Cathay. Odoric,
speaking of the wonders of Hangchow, refers for confirmation
to Venetian traders who have visited it: " 'Tis the greatest
city in the whole world, so great indeed that I should scarcely
venture to tell of it, but that I have met at Venice people in
plenty who have been there"; John of Monte Corvino was
accompanied by Master Peter of Lucolongo, "a great merchant," and John Marignolli mentions a *fondaco* for the use
of Christian merchants, which was attached to one
of the Franciscan convents at Zaiton. Above all, there is Francis Balducci Pegolotti, that intrepid factor who served the
great commercial house of the Bardi of Florence, and who
wrote a priceless handbook for the use of merchants about
1340. In this he gives detailed instructions for the guidance
of a merchant, who wishes to proceed from Tana on the Black
Sea by the overland route across Asia to Cathay and back again
with £12,000 worth of silk in his caravan, and remarks casually,
in passing, "The road you travel from Tana to Cathay is
perfectly safe, whether by day or night, according to what
merchants say who have used it"—"il chanmino dandare dalla
Tana al Ghattajo è *sichurissimo!*" [39] Think only of what it
all means. Marco Polo travelling where no man set foot again
till the twentieth century. The bells of the Christian church
ringing sweetly in the ears of the Great Khan in Peking. The
long road across Central Asia perfectly safe for merchants.
The "many persons at Venice" who have walked in the streets
of Hangchow. This is in the late thirteenth and early fourteenth centuries, in the despised and hidebound Middle Ages.
È *sichurissimo!* It takes some of the gilt off Columbus and
Vasco da Gama and the age (forsooth) of "discovery."

But a change came over everything in the middle of the
fourteenth century. Darkness fell again and swallowed up Peking and Hangchow, the great ports, the crowding junks, the
noble civilization. No longer was the great trade route
sichurissimo, and no longer did Christian friars chant their
Masses in Zaiton. The Tartar dynasty fell and the new rulers

of China reverted to the old anti-foreign policy; moreover, Islam spread its conquests all over Central Asia and lay like a rampart between the Far East and the West, a great wall of intolerance and hatred stronger by far than the great wall of stone which the Chinese had once built to keep out the Tartars. All Marco Polo's marvels became no more than a legend, a traveller's tale.

But that great adventurer was not done for yet. Nearly a century and a half after Marco's death a Genoese sea captain sat poring over one of the new printed books, which men were beginning to buy and to hand about among themselves. The book which he was reading was the Latin version of Marco Polo's travels. He was reading it with intentness and indeed with passion. As he read he made notes in the margin; on over seventy pages he made his notes.[40] From time to time he frowned and turned back and read again the tale of those great ports of Cathay and the gold-roofed palaces of Cipangu; and always he wondered how those lands might be reached, now that the wall of darkness covered Central Asia and anarchy blocked the road to the Persian Gulf. One day (may we not see him?) he lifted his head and smote his hand upon the table. "I will sail west," he said. "Maybe I shall find the lost island of Antilha in the western ocean, but maybe on its far rim I shall indeed come to Cipangu, for the world is round, and somewhere in those great seas beyond the coast of Europe must lie Marco Polo's rich Cathay. I will beseech the kings of England and of Spain for a ship and a ship's company, and the silk and the spices and the wealth shall be theirs. I will sail West," said the Genoese sea captain, and he smote his thigh. "I will sail West, West, West!" And this was the last of Messer Marco's marvels; he discovered China in the thirteenth century, when he was alive, and in the fifteenth, when he was dead, he discovered America!

CHAPTER III

MADAME EGLENTYNE

Chaucer's Prioress in Real Life

Ther was also a Nonne, a Prioresse,
That of hir smyling was ful simple and coy;
Hir grettest ooth was ne but by sëynt Loy;
And she was cleped madame Eglentyne.
Ful wel she song the service divyne,
Entuned in hir nose ful semely;
And Frensh she spak ful faire and fetisly,
After the scole of Stratford atte Bowe,
For Frensh of Paris was to hir unknowe.
At mete wel y-taught was she with-alle;
She leet no morsel from hir lippes falle,
Ne wette hir fingres in hir sauce depe.
Wel coude she carie a morsel and wel kepe,
That no drope ne fille up-on hir brest.
In curteisye was set ful muche hir lest.
Hir over lippe wyped she so clene,
That in hir coppe was no ferthing sene
Of grece, whan she dronken hadde hir draughte
Ful semely after hir mete she raughte,
And sikerly she was of greet disport,
And ful plesaunt and amiable of port,
And peyned hir to countrefete chere
Of court, and been estatlich of manere,
And to be holden digne of reverence.
But, for to speken of hir conscience,
She was so charitable and so pitous,
She wolde wepe, if that she sawe a mous
Caught in a trap, if it were deed or bledde.
Of smale houndes had she, that she fedde
With rosted flesh, or milk and wastel-breed
But sore wepe she if oon of hem were deed,

Or if men smoot it with a yerde smerte:
And al was conscience and tendre herte
Ful semely hir wimpel pinched was;
Hir nose tretys; hir eyen greye as glas;
Hir mouth ful smal, and ther-to softe and reed;
But sikerly she hadde a fair foreheed;
It was almost a spanne brood, I trowe;
For, hardily, she was nat undergrowe.
Ful fetis was hir cloke, as I was war.
Of smal coral aboute hir arm she bar
A peire of bedes, gauded al with grene;
And ther-on heng a broche of gold ful shene,
On which ther was first write a crowned A,
And after, *Amor vincit omnia!*
                    —GEOFFREY CHAUCER,
                              Prologue to the *Canterbury Tales*

EVERY one knows Chaucer's description of the Prioress, Madame Eglentyne, who rode with that very motley and talkative company on the way to Canterbury. There is no portrait in his gallery which has given rise to more diverse comment among critics. One interprets it as a cutting attack on the worldliness of the Church; another thinks that Chaucer meant to draw a charming and sympathetic picture of womanly gentleness; one says that it is a caricature, another an ideal; and an American professor even finds in it a psychological study of thwarted maternal instinct, apparently because Madame Eglentyne was fond of little dogs and told a story about a schoolboy. The mere historian may be excused from following these vagaries. To him Chaucer's Prioress, like Chaucer's monk and Chaucer's friar, will simply be one more instance of the almost photographic accuracy of the poet's observation. The rippling undercurrent of satire is always there; but it is Chaucer's own peculiar satire—mellow, amused, uncondemning, the most subtle kind of satire, which does not depend upon exaggeration. The literary critic has only Chaucer's words and his own heart, or sometimes (low be it spoken) his own desire to be original, by which to guide his judgment.

But the historian knows; he has all sorts of historical sources in which to study nunneries, and there he meets Chaucer's Prioress at every turn. Above all, he has the bishops' registers.

For a long time historians foolishly imagined that kings and wars and parliaments and the jury system alone were history; they liked chronicles and Acts of Parliament, and it did not strike them to go and look in dusty episcopal archives for the big books in which medieval bishops entered up the letters which they wrote and all the complicated business of running their dioceses. But when historians did think of looking there, they found a mine of priceless information about almost every side of social and ecclesiastical life. They had to dig for it of course, for almost all that is worth knowing has to be mined like precious metals out of a rock; and for one nugget the miner often has to grub for days underground in a mass of dullness; and when he has got it he has to grub in his own heart, or else he will not understand it. The historians found fine gold in the bishops' registers, when once they persuaded themselves that it was not beneath their dignity to grub there. They found descriptions of vicarages, with all their furniture and gardens; they found marriage disputes; they found wills full of entertaining legacies to people dead hundreds of years ago; they found excommunications; they found indulgences to men for relieving the poor, repairing roads, and building bridges, long before there was any poor law, or any county council; they found trials for heresy and witchcraft; they found accounts of miracles worked at the tombs of saints and even of some quite unsaintly people, such as Thomas of Lancaster, and Edward II, and Simon de Montfort; they found lists of travelling expenses when the bishops rode round their dioceses; in one they even found a minute account of the personal appearance of Queen Philippa, then a little girl at her father's Court at Hainault, whom the Bishop of Exeter had been sent to inspect, in order to see if she were pretty and good enough to marry Edward III: she was nine years old, and the bishop said that her second teeth were whiter than her first teeth and that her nose was broad but not snub, which was reassuring for Edward.[1] Last, but not least, the historians found a multitude of documents about monasteries, and among these documents they found visitation records, and among visitation records they found Chaucer's Prioress, smiling full simple and coy, fair forehead, well-pinched wimple, necklace, little dogs, and all, as though she had stepped into a stuffy register by mistake for the "Canterbury Tales" and was longing to get out again.

This was the reason that Madame Eglentyne got into the register. In the Middle Ages all the nunneries of England, and a great many of the monasteries, used to be visited at intervals by the bishop of their diocese—or by somebody sent by him—in order to see whether they were behaving properly. It was rather like the periodical visitation of a school by one of His Majesty's inspectors, only what happened was very different. When His Majesty's inspector comes he does not sit in state in the hall, and call all the inmates in front of him one after another, from the head mistress to the smallest child in the first form, and invite them to say in what way they think the school is not being properly run, and what complaints they have to make against their mistresses and which girl habitually breaks the rules—all breathed softly and privately into his ear, with no one to overhear them. But when the bishop came to visit a nunnery, that is precisely what happened. First of all, he sent a letter to say he was coming, and to bid the nuns prepare for him. Then he came, with his clerks and a learned official or two, and was met solemnly by the prioress and all the nuns, and preached a sermon in their church, and was entertained, perhaps, to dinner. And then he prepared to examine them, and one by one they came before him, in order of rank, beginning with the prioress, and what they had to do was to tell tales about each other. He wanted to find out if the prioress were ruling well, and if the services were properly performed, and if the finances were in good order, and if discipline were maintained; and if any nun had a complaint, then was the time to make it.

And the nuns were full of complaints. A modern schoolgirl would go pale with horror over their capacity for tale-bearing. If one nun had boxed her sister's ears, if another had cut church, if another were too much given to entertaining friends, if another went out without a licence, if another had run away with a wandering fluteplayer, the bishop was sure to hear about it; that is, unless the whole convent were in a disorderly state, and the nuns had made a compact to wink at each other's peccadilloes; and not to betray them to the bishop, which occasionally happened. And if the prioress were at all unpopular he was quite certain to hear all about her. "She fares splendidly in her own room and never invites us," says one nun; "She has favourites," says another, "and when she makes corrections she passes lightly over those whom she likes, and speedily punishes those whom she dislikes"; "She is a fearful scold," says a third; "She dresses more like a secular person than a nun, and wears rings and necklaces," says a fourth; "She goes out riding to see her friends far too often," says a fifth; "She-is-a-very-bad-business-woman-and-she-has-let-the-house-get-into-debt-and-the-church-is-falling-about-our-ears-and-we-don't-get-enough-food-and-she-hasn't-given-us-any-clothes-for-two-years-and-she-has-sold-woods-and-farms-without-your-licence-and-she-has-pawned-our-best-set-of-spoons; and no wonder, when she never consults us in any business as she ought to do." They go on like that for pages, and the bishop must often have wanted to put his fingers in his ears and shout to them to stop; especially as the prioress had probably spent half an hour, for her part, in telling him how disobedient and ill-tempered, and thoroughly badly behaved the nuns were.

All these tales the bishop's clerk solemnly wrote down in a big book, and when the examination was over the bishop summoned all the nuns together again. And if they had answered "All is well," as they sometimes did, or only mentioned trivial faults, he commended them and went his way; and if they had shown that things really were in a bad way, he investigated particular charges and scolded the culprits and ordered them to amend, and when he got back to his palace, or the manor where he was staying, he wrote out a set of injunctions, based on the complaints, and saying exactly how things were to be improved; and of these injunctions one copy was entered in his register and another was sent by hand to the nuns, who were supposed to read it aloud at intervals and to obey everything in it. We have in many bishops' registers these lists of injunctions, copied into them by the bishops' clerks, and in some, notably in a splendid fifteenth-century Lincoln register, belonging to the good bishop Alnwick, we have also the evidence of the nuns, just as it was taken down from their chattering mouths, and these are the most human and amusing of all medieval records. It is easy to see what important historical documents visitation reports are, especially in a diocese like Lincoln, which possesses an almost unbroken series of registers, ranging over the three centuries before the Dissolution, so that one can trace the whole history of some of the nunneries by the successive visitations.

Let us see what light the registers will throw upon Madame Eglentyne, before Chaucer observed her mounting her horse outside the Tabard Inn. Doubtless she first came to the nunnery when she was quite a little girl, because girls counted as grown up when they were fifteen in the Middle Ages; they could be married out of hand at twelve, and they could become nuns for ever at fourteen. Probably Eglentyne's father had three other daughters to marry, each with a dowry, and a gay young spark of a son, who spent a lot of money on fashionable suits,

> Embroidered . . . as it were a mede
> All ful of fresshe flowers white and rede.

So he thought he had better settle the youngest at once; and he got together a dowry (it was rarely possible to get into a nunnery without one, though Church law really forbade anything except voluntary offerings), and, taking Eglentyne by the hand one summer day, he popped her into a nunnery a few miles off, which had been founded by his ancestors. We may even know what it cost him; it was rather a select, aristocratic house, and he had to pay an entrance fee of £200 in modern money; and then he had to give Eglentyne her new habit and a bed, and some other furniture; and he had to make a feast on the day she became a nun, and invite all the nuns

and all his own friends; and he had to tip the friar, who
preached the sermon; and, altogether, it was a great affair.[2]
But the feast would not come at once, because Eglentyne
would have to remain a novice for some years, until she were
old enough to take the vows. So she would stay in the convent
and be taught how to sing and to read, and to talk French
of the school of Stratford-atte-Bowe with the other novices.
Perhaps she was the youngest, for girls often did not enter
the convent until they were old enough to decide for themselves whether they wanted to be nuns; but there were certainly some other quite tiny novices learning their lessons;
and occasionally there would be a little girl like the one whose
sad fate is recorded in a dull law-book, shut up in a nunnery
by a wicked stepfather who wanted her inheritance (a nun
could not inherit land, because she was supposed to be dead
to the world), and told by the nuns that the devil would fly
away with her if she tried to set foot outside the door.[3] However, Eglentyne had a sunny disposition, and liked life in
the nunnery, and had a natural aptitude for the pretty table
manners which she learnt there, as well as for talking French,
and though she was not at all prim and liked the gay clothes
and pet dogs which she used to see at home in her mother's
bower, still she had no hesitation at all about taking the veil
when she was fifteen, and indeed she rather liked the fuss
that was made of her, and being called *Madame* or *Dame*,
which was the courtesy title always given to a nun.

The years passed and Eglentyne's life jogged along peacefully enough behind the convent walls. The great purpose for
which the nunneries existed, and which most of them fulfilled
not unworthily, was the praise of God. Eglentyne spent a
great deal of her time singing and praying in the convent
church, and, as we know,

> Ful wel she song the service divyne,
> Entuned in hir nose ful semely.

The nuns had seven monastic offices to say every day. About
2 a.m. the night office was said; they all got out of bed when
the bell rang, and went down in the cold and the dark to the

church choir and said Matins, followed immediately by Lauds. Then they went back to bed, just as the dawn was breaking in the sky, and slept again for three hours, and then got up for good at six o'clock and said Prime. After that there followed Tierce, Sext, None, Vespers, and Compline, spread at intervals through the day. The last service, compline, was said at 7 p.m. in winter, and at 8 p.m. in summer, after which the nuns were supposed to go straight to bed in the dorter, in which connexion one Nun's Rule ordains that "None shall push up against another wilfully, nor spit upon the stairs going up and down, but if they tread it out forthwith"![4] They had in all about eight hours' sleep, broken in the middle by the night service. They had three meals, a light repast of bread and beer after prime in the morning, a solid dinner to the accompaniment of reading aloud in the middle of the day, and a short supper immediately after vespers at 5 or 6 p.m.

From 12 to 5 p.m. in winter and from 1 to 6 p.m. in summer Eglentyne and her sisters were supposed to devote themselves to manual or brain work, interspersed with a certain amount of sober and godly recreation. She would spin, or embroider vestments with the crowned monogram M of the Blessed Virgin in blue and gold thread, or make little silken purses for her friends and finely sewn bands for them to bind round their arms after a bleeding. She would read too, in her psalter or in such saints' lives as the convent possessed, written in French or English; for her Latin was weak, though she could construe "Amor vincit omnia." Perhaps her convent took in a few little schoolgirls to learn their letters and good manners with the nuns, and when she grew older she helped to teach them to read and sing; for though they were happy, they did not receive a very extensive education from the good sisters. In the summer Eglentyne was sometimes allowed to work in the convent garden, or even to go out haymaking with the other nuns; and came back round-eyed to confide in her confessor that she had seen the cellaress returning therefrom seated behind the chaplain on his nag,[5] and had thought what fun it must be to jog behind stout Dan John.

Except for certain periods of relaxation strict silence was supposed to be observed in the convent for a large part of the day, and if Eglentyne desired to communicate with her sisters, she was urged to do so by means of signs. The persons who drew up the lists of signs which were in use in medieval monastic houses, however, combined a preternatural ingenuity with an extremely exiguous sense of humour, and the sort of dumb pandemonium which went on at Eglentyne's dinner table must often have been more mirth-provoking than speech. The sister who desired fish would "wag her hands displayed sidelings in manner of a fish tail"; she who wanted milk would "draw her left little finger in manner of milking"; for mustard one would "hold her nose in the upper part of her right fist and rub it"; another for salt would "fillip with her right thumb and forefinger over the left thumb"; another desirous of wine would "move her forefinger up and down the end of her thumb afore her eye"; and the guilty sacristan, struck by the thought that she had not provided incense for the Mass, would "put her two fingers into her nostrils." In one such table drawn up for nuns there are no less than 106 signs, and on the whole it is not surprising that the rule of the same nuns enjoins that "it is never lawful to use them without some reason and profitable need, for oft-times more hurt hath an evil word, and more offence it may be to God." [6]

The nuns, of course, would not have been human if they had not sometimes grown a little weary of all these services and this silence; for the religious life was not, nor was it intended to be, an easy one. It was not a mere means of escape from work and responsibility. In the early golden age of monasticism only men and women with a vocation, that is to say a real genius for monastic life, entered convents. Moreover, when there they worked very hard with hand and brain, as well as with soul, and so they got variety of occupation, which is as good as a holiday. The basis of wise St. Benedict's Rule was a nicely adjusted combination of variety with regularity; for he knew human nature. Thus monks and nuns did not find the services monotonous, and indeed regarded them as by far the best part of the day. But in the later Middle Ages, when Chaucer lived, young people had begun to enter monastic houses rather as a profession than as a vocation. Many truly spiritual men and women still took the vows, but with them came others who were little suited to monastic life, and who lowered its standard, because it was hard and uncongenial to them. Eglentyne became a nun because her father did not want the trouble and expense of finding her a husband, and because being a nun was about the only career for a well-born lady who did not marry. Moreover, by this time, monks and nuns had grown more lazy, and did little work with their hands and still less with their heads, particularly in nunneries, where the early tradition of learning had died out and where many nuns could hardly understand the Latin in which their services were written. The result was that monastic life began to lose that essential variety which St. Benedict had designed for it, and as a result the regularity sometimes became irksome, and the series of services degenerated into a mere routine of peculiar monotony, which many of the singers could no longer keep alive with spiritual fervour. Thus sometimes (it must not be imagined that this happened in all or even in the majority of houses) the services became empty forms, to be hurried through with scant devotion and occasionally with scandalous irreverence. It was the almost inevitable reaction from too much routine.

Carelessness in the performance of the monastic hours was an exceedingly common fault during the later Middle Ages, though the monks were always worse about it than the nuns. Sometimes they "cut" the services. Sometimes they behaved with the utmost levity, as at Exeter in 1330, where the canons giggled and joked and quarrelled during the services and dropped hot candle wax from the upper stalls on to the shaven heads of the singers in the stalls below! [7] Sometimes they came late to matins, in the small hours after midnight. This fault was common in nunneries, for the nuns always would insist on having private drinkings and gossipings in the evening after compline, instead of going straight to bed, as the rule demanded—a habit which did not conduce to wakefulness at 1 a.m. Consequently they were somewhat sleepy at matins and found an almost Johnsonian difficulty in getting up early. Wise St. Benedict foresaw the difficulty, when he wrote in his rule: "When they rise for the Divine Office, let them gently encourage one another, because of the excuses made by those that are drowsy." [8] At the nunnery of Stainfield in 1519 the bishop discovered that half an hour sometimes elapsed between the last stroke of the bell and the beginning of the service, and that some of the nuns did not sing, but dozed, partly because they had not enough candles, but chiefly because they went late to bed;[9] and whoever is without sin among us, let him cast the first stone! There was a tendency also among both monks and nuns to slip out before the end of the service on any good or bad excuse: they had to see after the dinner or the guest-house, their gardens needed weeding, or they did not feel well. But the most common fault of all was to gabble through the services as quickly as they could in order to get them over. They left out the syllables at the beginning and end of words, they omitted the dipsalma or pause between two verses, so that one side of the choir was beginning the second half before the other side had finished the first; they skipped sentences, they mumbled and slurred what should have been "entuned in their nose ful semely," and altogether they made a terrible mess of the stately plain-song. So prevalent was the fault of gabbling that the Father of Evil was obliged to charter a special Devil called Tittivillus, whose sole business it was to collect all these dropped syllables and carry them back to his master in a big bag. In one way or another, we have a good deal of information about him, for he was always letting himself be seen by holy men, who generally had a sharp eye for devils. One Latin rhyme distinguishes carefully between the contents of his sack: "These are they who wickedly corrupt the holy psalms: the dangler, the gasper, the leaper, the galloper, the dragger, the mumbler, the fore-skipper, the fore-runner and the over-leaper: Tittivillus collecteth the fragments of these men's words." [10] Indeed, a holy Cistercian abbot once interviewed the poor little devil himself and heard about his alarming industry; this is the story as it is told in *The Myroure of Oure Ladye*, written for the delectation of the nuns of Syon in the fifteenth century: "We read of a holy Abbot of the order of Citeaux that while he stood in the choir at matins he saw a fiend that had a long and great poke hanging about his neck and went about the choir from one to another and waited busily after all letters and syllables and words and failings that any made; and them he gathered diligently and put them in his poke. And when he came before the Abbot, waiting if aught had escaped him that he might have gotten and put in his bag, the Abbot was astonied and afeard of the foulness and misshape of him and said unto him: What art thou? And he answered and said, I am a poor devil and my name is Tittivillus and I do mine office that is committed unto me. And what is thine office? said the Abbot. He answered: I must each day, he said, bring my master a thousand pokes full of failings and of negligences and syllables and words, that are done in your order in reading and singing and else I must be sore beaten." [11] But there is no reason to suppose that he often got his beating, though one may be sure that Madame Eglentyne, busily chanting through her nose, never gave him the slightest help. In his spare moments, when he was not engaged in picking up those unconsidered trifles which the monks let fall from the psalms, Tittivillus used to fill up odd corners of his sack with the idle talk of people who gossiped in church; and he also sat up aloft and collected all the high notes of vain tenors, who sang to their own glory, instead of to the glory of God, and pitched the chants three notes higher than the cracked voices of their elders could rise.

But the monotony of convent life sometimes did more than make the nuns unconscious contributors to Tittivillus's sack. It sometimes played havoc with their tempers. The nuns were not chosen for convent life because they were saints. They were no more immune from tantrums than was the Wife of Bath, who was out of all charity when other village wives went into church before her; and sometimes they got terribly on each others' nerves. Readers of *Piers Plowman*, will remember that when the seven deadly sins come in, Wrath tells how he was cook to the prioress of a convent and, says he,

Of wycked wordes I, Wrath . here wordes imade,
Til "thow lixte" and "thow lixte" . lopen oute at ones,
And eyther hitte other . vnder the cheke;
Hadde thei had knyves, by Cryst . her eyther had killed
    other.

To be sure, it is not often that we hear of anything so bad
as that fifteenth-century prioress, who used to drag her nuns
round the choir by their veils in the middle of the service,
screaming "Liar!" and "Harlot!" at them;[12] or that other
sixteenth-century lady who used to kick them and hit them
on the head with her fists and put them in the stocks.[13] All
prioresses were not "ful plesaunt and amiable of port," or
stately in their manner. The records of monastic visitations
show that bad temper and petty bickering sometimes broke
the peace of convent life.

But we must be back at Eglentyne. She went on living for
ten or twelve years as a simple nun, and she sang the services
very nicely and had a sweet temper and pretty manners and
was very popular. Moreover, she was of good birth; Chaucer
tells us a great deal about her beautiful behaviour at table
and her courtesy, which shows that she was a lady born and
bred; indeed, his description of this might have been taken
straight out of one of the feudal books of deportment for
girls; even her personal beauty—straight nose, grey eyes and
little red mouth—conforms to the courtly standard. The convents were apt to be rather snobbish; ladies and rich burgesses' daughters got into them, but poor and low-born girls
never. So the nuns probably said to each other that what with
her pretty ways and her good temper and her aristocratic con-
nexions, wouldn't it be a good thing to choose her for prioress
when the old prioress died? And so they did, and she had been
a prioress for some years when Chaucer met her. At first it
was very exciting, and Eglentyne liked being called "Mother"
by nuns who were older than herself, and having a private
room to sit in and all the visitors to entertain. But she soon
found that it was not by any means all a bed of roses; for
there was a great deal of business to be done by the head of a

house—not only looking after the internal discipline of the
convent, but also superintending money matters and giving
orders to the bailiffs on her estates, and seeing that the farms
were paying well, and the tithes coming in to the churches
which belonged to the nunnery, and that the Italian merchants
who came to buy the wool off her sheeps' backs gave a good
price for it. In all this business she was supposed to take the
advice of the nuns, meeting in the chapterhouse, where all
business was transacted. I am afraid that sometimes Eglentyne
used to think that it was much better to do things by herself,
and so she would seal documents with the convent seal without telling them. One should always distrust the head of an
office or school or society who says, with a self-satisfied air,
that it is much more satisfactory to do the thing herself than
to depute it to the proper subordinates; it either means that
she is an autocrat, or else that she cannot organize. Madame
Eglentyne was rather an autocrat, in a good-natured sort of
way, and besides she hated bother. So she did not always
consult the nuns; and I fear too (after many researches into
that past of hers which Chaucer forgot to mention) that she
often tried to evade rendering an account of income and
expenditure to them every year, as she was supposed to do.

The nuns, of course, objected to this; and the first time the
bishop came on his rounds they complained about it to him.
They said, too, that she was a bad business woman and got
into debt; and that when she was short of money she used to
sell woods belonging to the convent, and promise annual pen-
sions to various people in return for lump sums down, and
lease out farms for a long time at low rates, and do various
other things by which the convent would lose in the long run.
And besides, she had let the roof of the church get into such
ill repair that rain came through the holes on to their heads
when they were singing; and would my lord bishop please to
look at the holes in their clothes and tell her to provide them
with new ones? Other wicked prioresses used sometimes even
to pawn the plate and jewels of the convent, to get money
for their own private purposes. But Eglentyne was not at all
wicked or dishonest, though she was a bad manager; the fact

was that she had no head for figures. I am *sure* that she had
no head for figures; you have only got to read Chaucer's description of her to know that she was not a mathematician.
Besides the nuns were exaggerating: their clothes were not
in holes, only just a little threadbare. Madame Eglentyne was
far too fastidious to allow ragged clothes about her; and as
to the roof of the church, she had meant to save enough money
to have some tiles put on to it, but it really *was* very hard to
make two ends meet in a medieval nunnery, especially if (as
I repeat) you had no head for figures. Probably the bishop saw
how the land lay, so he ordered her never to do anything
without consulting the convent, and he shut up the common
seal in a box with three different sorts of locks, to which
Madame Eglentyne and two of the senior nuns had the keys,
so that she could not open it alone and so could not seal any
business agreement without their consent. And he ordered
her to keep accounts and present them every year (there are
bundles of her accounts still preserved in the Record Office).
Finally he deputed a neighbouring rector to act as custodian
of the business affairs of the house so that she should always
have his help. Things went better after that.

Eglentyne, it seems, was never really interested in business,
and was quite pleased to have her time taken up with looking
after internal affairs and entertaining visitors, with an occasional jaunt outside to see how the estates were getting on.
And she began to find that she could lead a much freer and
gayer life now that she was a prioress; for the prioress of a
convent had rooms of her own, instead of sharing the common
dormitory and refectory; sometimes she even had a sort of
little house with a private kitchen. The abbess of one great
nunnery at Winchester in the sixteenth century had her own
staff to look after her, a cook, and an under cook, and a housemaid and a gentlewoman to wait upon her, like any great lady
in the world, and never dined with the nuns except on state
occasions. But a superior generally had with her one nun to
act as her companion and assist her in the choir and be a
witness to her good behaviour; this nun was called her chaplain, and was supposed to be changed every year, to prevent

favouritism. It will be remembered that when Madame Eglentyne went on her pilgrimage she took her nun chaplain with her, as well as three priests; that was because no nun was ever allowed to go out alone. One of Madame Eglentyne's duties as prioress was to entertain visitors with her celebrated cheer of court, and we may be sure that she had a great many. Her sisters, who were now grand ladies with husbands and manors of their own, and her old father, and all the great people of the county came to congratulate her; and after that they used often to drop in for a dinner of chickens and wine and wastel bread, if they passed the house on a journey, and sometimes they spent the night there. One or two ladies, whose husbands were away at the wars or on a pilgrimage to Rome, even came as paying guests to the convent and lived there for a whole year, for nothing pleased the country gentlemen or wealthy burgesses better than to use nunneries as boarding-houses for their women-kind.

All this was very disturbing to the peace and quiet of the nuns, and especially disturbing were the boarders, for they wore gay clothes, and had pet dogs and callers, and set a very frivolous example to the nuns. At one nunnery we find a bishop ordering: "Let Felmersham's wife, with her whole household and other women, be utterly removed from your monastery within one year, seeing that they are a cause of disturbance to the nuns and an occasion to bad example, by reason of their attire and of those who come to visit them." [14] It can be easily imagined *why* the bishops objected so much to the reception of these worldly married women as boarders. Just substitute for "Felmersham's wife" "the Wife of Bath" and all is explained. That lady was not a person whom a prioress would lightly refuse; the list of her pilgrimages alone would give her the *entrée* into any nunnery. Smiling her gap-toothed smile and riding easily upon her ambler, she would enter the gates, and what a month of excitement would pass before she rode away again. I am sure that it was she who taught Madame Eglentyne the most fashionable way to pinch a wimple; and she certainly introduced hats "as broad as is a buckler or a targe" and scarlet stockings into some nunneries. The bishops

disliked it all very much, but they never succeeded in turning
the boarders out for all their efforts, because the nuns always
needed the money which they paid for their board and lodging.

It is easy to understand that this constant intercourse with
worldly visitors would give rise to the spread of worldly habits
in Madame Eglentyne's nunnery. Nuns, after all, were but
women, and they had the amiable vanities of their sex. But
Authority (with a large A) did not consider their vanities
amiable at all. It was the view of Authority that the Devil had
dispatched three lesser D's to be the damnation of nuns, and
those three D's were Dances, Dresses, and Dogs. Medieval
England was famous for dancing and mumming and min-
strelsy; it was Merry England because, however plague and
pestilence and famine and the cruelties of man to man might
darken life, still it loved these things. But there were no two
views possible about what the Church thought of dancing; it
was accurately summed up by one moralist in the aphorism,
"the Devil is the inventor and governor and disposer of dances
and dancing." Yet when we look into those accounts which
Madame Eglentyne rendered (or did not render) to her nuns
at the end of every year, we shall find payments for wassail at
New Year and Twelfth Night, for May games, for bread and
ale on bonfire nights, for harpers and players at Christmas, for
a present to the Boy Bishop on his rounds, and perhaps for an
extra pittance when the youngest schoolgirl was allowed to
dress up and act as abbess of the convent for the whole of
Innocents' Day. And when we look in the bishops' registers we
shall find Madame Eglentyne forbidden "all manner of min-
strelsy, interludes, dancing or revelling within your holy
place"; and she would be fortunate indeed if her bishop would
make exception for Christmas, "and other honest times of recreation among yourselves used in absence of seculars in all
wise." Somehow one feels an insistent conviction that her cheer
of court included dancing.[15]

Then, again, there were the fashionable dresses which the
visitors introduced into nunneries. It is quite certain that Madame Eglentyne was not unmoved by them; and it is a sad fact

that she began to think the monastic habit very black and
ugly, and the monastic life very strict; and to decide that if
some little amenities were imported into it no one would be
a penny the worse, and perhaps the bishop would not notice.
That is why, when Chaucer met her,

> Ful fetis was hir cloke, as I was war,
> Of smal coral aboute hir arm she bar
> A peire of bedes, gauded al with grene,
> And ther-on heng a broche of gold ful shene.

Unfortunately, however, the bishop did notice; the registers
are indeed full of those clothes of Madame Eglentyne's, and
of the even more frivolous ones which she wore in the privacy
of the house. For more than six weary centuries the bishops
waged a holy war against fashion in the cloister, and waged it
in vain; for as long as nuns mingled freely with secular women,
it was impossible to prevent them from adopting secular
modes. Occasionally a wretched bishop would find himself
floundering unhandily, in masculine bewilderment, through
something like a complete catalogue of contemporary fashions,
in order to specify what the nuns were *not* to wear. Synods sat
solemnly, bishops and archbishops shook their grey heads, over
golden hairpins and silver belts, jewelled rings, laced shoes,
slashed tunics, low necks and long trains, gay colours, costly
cloth and valuable furs. The nuns were supposed to wear their
veils pinned tightly down to their eyebrows, so that their foreheads were completely hidden; but high foreheads happened
to be fashionable among worldly ladies, who even shaved
theirs to make them higher, and the result was that the nuns
could not resist lifting up and spreading out their veils, for how
otherwise did Chaucer *know* that Madame Eglentyne had such
a fair forehead ("almost a spanne broad, I trowe")? If she had
been wearing her veil properly, it would have been invisible,
and the father of English poetry may be observed discreetly
but plainly winking the other eye when he puts in that little
touch; his contemporaries would see the point very quickly.
And that brooch and that fetis cloak of hers. . . . Here is
what some tale-bearing nuns told the Bishop of Lincoln about

their Prioress, fifty years after Chaucer wrote the *Canterbury Tales*. "The Prioress," they said with their most sanctimonious air, "wears golden rings exceeding costly, with divers precious stones and also girdles silvered and gilded over and silken veils and she carries her veil too high above her forehead, so that her forehead, being entirely uncovered, can be seen of all, and she wears furs of vair. Also she wears shifts of cloth of Rennes, which costs sixteen pence the ell. Also she wears kirtles laced with silk and tiring pins of silver and silver gilt and has made all the nuns wear the like. Also she wears above her veil a cap of estate, furred with budge. Item, she has on her neck a long silken band, in English a lace, which hangs down below her breast and there on a golden ring with one diamond." [16] Is it not Madame Eglentyne to the life? Nothing escaped our good Dan Chaucer's eye, for all that he rode always looking on the ground.

Moreover, it was not only in her dress that the Prioress and her sister nuns aped the fashions of the world. Great ladies of the day loved to amuse themselves with pet animals; and nuns were quick to follow their example. So,

> Of smale houndes had she, that she fedde
> With rosted flesh, or milk and wastel-breed.
> But sore weep she if oon of hem were deed,
> Or if men smoot it with a yerde smerte.

The visitation reports are full of those little dogs and other animals; and how many readers of the Prologue know that the smale houndes, like the fair forehead and the brooch of gold full sheen, were strictly against the rules? For the bishops regarded pets as bad for discipline, and century after century they tried to turn the animals out of the convents, without the slightest success. The nuns just waited till the bishop had gone and then whistled their dogs back again. Dogs were easily the favourite pets, though monkeys, squirrels, rabbits, birds and (very rarely) cats were also kept. One archbishop had to forbid an abbess whom he visited to keep *monkeys and a number of dogs* in her own chamber and charged her at the same time with stinting her nuns in food; one can guess what be-

came of the roasted flesh or milk and wastel-breed! It was a
common medieval practice to bring animals into church, where
ladies often attended service with dog in lap and men with
hawk on wrist; just as the highland farmer brings his collie
with him to-day. This happened in the nunneries too. Sometimes it was the lay-boarders in the convents who brought their
pets with them; there is a pathetic complaint by the nuns of
one house "that Lady Audley, who boards there, has a great
abundance of dogs, insomuch that whenever she comes to
church there follow her twelve dogs, who make a great uproar
in church, hindering the nuns in their psalmody and the nuns
thereby are terrified!" [17] But often enough the nuns themselves transgressed. Injunctions against bringing pet dogs into
choir occur in several visitation reports, the most amusing instance being contained in those sent to Romsey Abbey by
William of Wykeham in 1387, just about the same year that
Chaucer was writing the *Canterbury Tales*: "Item," runs the
injunction, "whereas we have convinced ourselves by clear
proofs that some of the nuns of your house bring with them to
church birds, rabbits, hounds and such like frivolous things,
whereunto they give more heed than to the offices of the
church, with frequent hindrance to their own psalmody and to
that of their fellow nuns and to the grievous peril of their
souls—therefor we strictly forbid you all and several, in virtue
of the obedience due to us that ye presume henceforward to
bring to church no birds, hounds, rabbits or other frivolous
things that promote indiscipline. . . . Item, whereas through
hunting dogs and other hounds abiding within your monastic
precincts, the alms that should be given to the poor are de-
voured and the church and cloister . . . are foully defiled
. . . and whereas, through their inordinate noise divine service
is frequently troubled—therefore we strictly command and en-
join you, Lady Abbess, that you remove the dogs altogether
and that you suffer them never henceforth, nor any other such
hounds, to abide within the precincts of your nunnery." [18]
But it was useless for any bishop to order Madame Eglentyne
to give up her dogs, she could not even be parted from them on

a pilgrimage, though they must have been a great nuisance in the inns, especially as she was so fussy about their food.

For Chaucer's prioress, we must admit, was rather a worldly lady, though her pretty clothes and little dogs were harmless enough on modern standards and one's sympathies are all against the bishops. She probably became more worldly as time went on, because she had so many opportunities for social intercourse. Not only had she to entertain visitors in the convent, but often the business of the house took her away upon journeys and these offered many opportunities for hobnobbing with her neighbours. Sometimes she had to go to London to see after a law-suit and that was a great excursion with another nun, or perhaps two, and a priest and several yeomen to look after her. Sometimes she had to go and see the bishop, to get permission to take in some little schoolgirls. Sometimes she went to the funeral of a great man, whom her father knew and who left her twenty shillings and a silver cup in his will. Sometimes she went to the wedding of one of her sisters, or to be godmother to their babies; though the bishops did not like these worldly ties, or the dances and merry-makings which accompanied weddings and christenings. Indeed her nuns occasionally complained about her journeys and said that though she pretended it was all on the business of the house, they had their doubts; and would the bishop please just look into it. At one nunnery we find the nuns complaining that their house is £20 in debt "and this principally owing to the costly expenses of the prioress, because she frequently rides abroad and pretends that she does so on the common business of the house although it is not so, with a train of attendants much too large and tarries too long abroad and she feasts sumptuously, both when abroad and at home and she is very choice in her dress, so that the fur trimmings of her mantle are worth 100s"! [19]

As a matter of fact there was nothing of which the church disapproved more than this habit, shared by monks and nuns, of wandering about outside their cloisters; moralists considered that intercourse with the world was at the root of all the evil which crept into the monastic system. The orthodox saying was that a monk out of his cloister was like a fish out of water; and it will be remembered that Chaucer's monk thought the text not worth an oyster. Indeed most of the monks managed to swim very well in the air, and the nuns too persisted in taking every sort of excuse for wandering in the world. Right through the Middle Ages council after council, bishop after bishop, reformer after reformer, tried in vain to keep them shut up. The greatest attempt of all began in 1300, when the pope published a Bull ordering that nuns should never, save in very exceptional circumstances, leave their convents and that no secular person should be allowed to go in and visit them, without a special licence and a good reason. This will make the modern reader pity the poor nuns, but there is no need, for nobody ever succeeded in putting it into force for more than five minutes, though the bishops spent over two centuries in trying to do so and were still trying in vain when King Henry VIII dissolved the nunneries and turned all the nuns out into the world for ever, whether they liked it or not. At one nunnery in the Lincoln diocese, when the bishop came and deposited a copy of the Bull in the house and ordered the nuns to obey it, they ran after him to the gate when he was riding away and threw the Bull at his head, screaming that they would never observe it.[20] The more practical bishops indeed, soon stopped trying to enforce the Bull as it stood and contented themselves with ordering that nuns were not to go out or pay visits too often, or without a companion, or without licence, or without a good reason. But even in this they were not very successful, because the nuns were most prolific in excellent reasons why they should go out. Sometimes they said that their parents were ill; and then they would go away to smooth the pillow of the sick. Sometimes they said that they had to go to market to buy herrings. Sometimes they said that they had to go to confession at a monastery. Sometimes it is really difficult to imagine *what* they said. What are we to think, for instance of that giddy nun "who on Monday night did pass the night with the Austin friars at Northampton and did dance and play the lute with them in the same place until midnight, and on the night following she passed the night with the Friars' preachers at Northamp-

ton, luting and dancing in like manner"? [21] Chaucer told us
how the friar loved harping and how his eyes twinkled like
stars in his head when he sang, but failed perhaps to observe
that he had lured Madame Eglentyne into a dance.

It is indeed difficult to see what "legitimate" excuses the
nuns can have made for all their wandering about in the streets
and the fields and in and out of people's houses, and it is
sorely to be feared that either they were too much of a handful
for Madame Eglentyne, or else she winked at their doings. For
somehow or other one suspects that she had no great opinion
of bishops. After all Chaucer would never have met her, if
she had not managed to circumvent her own, since if there was
one excuse for wandering of which the bishops thoroughly
disapproved, it was precisely the excuse of pilgrimages. Madame Eglentyne was not quite as simple and coy as she looked.
How many of the literary critics, who chuckle over her, know
that she never ought to have got into the Prologue at all? The
Church was quite clear in its mind that pilgrimages for nuns
were to be discouraged. As early as 791 a council had forbidden the practice and in 1195 another at York decreed, "In
order that the opportunity of wandering may be taken from
nuns we forbid them to take the path of pilgrimage." In 1318
an archbishop of York strictly forbade the nuns of one convent to leave their house "by reason of any vow of pilgrimage
which they might have taken. If any had taken such vows she
was to say as many psalters as it would have taken days to
perform the pilgrimage so rashly vowed." [22] One has a melan-
choly vision of poor Madame Eglentyne saying psalters inter-
minably through her tretys nose, instead of jogging along so
gaily with her motley companions and telling so prettily her
tale of little St. Hugh. Such prohibitions might be multiplied
from medieval records; and indeed it is unnecessary to go further than Chaucer to understand why it was that bishops
offered such strenuous opposition to pilgrimages for nuns; one
has only to remember some of the folk, in whose company the
prioress travelled and some of the tales they told. If one could
only be certain, for instance, that she rode all the time with
her nun and her priests, or at least between the Knight and

and the poor Parson of a town! But there were also the Miller and the Summoner and (worst of all) that cheerful and engaging sinner, the Wife of Bath. It is really quite disturbing to think what additional details the Wife of Bath may have given the prioress about her five husbands.

This then was Chaucer's prioress in real life, for the poet who drew her was one of the most wonderful observers in the whole of English literature. We may wade through hundreds of visitation reports and injunctions and everywhere the grey eyes of his prioress will twinkle at us out of their pages, and in the end we must always go to Chaucer for her picture, to sum up everything that historical records have taught us. As the bishop found her, so he saw her, aristocratic, tender-hearted, worldly, taking pains to "countrefete chere of court"; liking pretty clothes and little dogs; a lady of importance, attended by a nun and three priests; spoken to with respect by the none too mealy-mouthed host—no "by Corpus Dominus" or "cokkes bones" or "tel on a devel wey" for her, but "cometh neer, my lady prioress," and

> My lady Prioresse, by your leve
> If that I wiste I sholde yow nat greve,
> I wolde demen that ye tellen sholde
> A tale next, if so were that ye wolde.
> Now wol ye vouche-sauf, my lady dere?

He talks to no one else like that, save perhaps to the knight. Was she religious? Perhaps; but save for her singing the divine service and for her lovely address to the Virgin, at the beginning of her tale, Chaucer can find but little to say on the point;

> But for to speken of hir conscience (he says)
> She was so charitable and so pitous,

and then, as we are waiting to hear of her almsgiving to the poor—that she would weep over a mouse in a trap, or a beaten puppy, says Chaucer. A good ruler of her house? again, doubtless. But when Chaucer met her the house was ruling itself somewhere at the "shire's ende." The world was full of fish out

of water in the fourteenth century, and, by sëynt Loy, said
Madame Eglentyne, swearing her greatest oath, like Chaucer's
monk, she held that famous text not worth an oyster. So we
take our leave of her, characteristically on the road to Canterbury.

CHAPTER IV

THE MÉNAGIER'S WIFE

A Paris Housewife in the Fourteenth Century

The sphere of woman is the home.
—*Homo Sapiens*

THE men of the middle, as indeed of all ages, including our own, were very fond of writing books of deportment telling women how they ought to behave in all the circumstances of their existence, but more particularly in their relations with their husbands. Many of these books have survived, and among them one which is of particular interest, because of the robust good sense of its writer and the intimate and lively picture which it gives of a bourgeois home. Most books of deportment were written, so to speak, in the air, for women in general, but this was written by a particular husband for a particular wife, and thus is drawn from life and full of detail, showing throughout an individuality which its compeers too often lack. If a parallel be sought to it, it is perhaps to be found not in any other medieval treatise but in those passages of Xenophon's *Economist*, in which Isomachus describes to Socrates the training of a perfect Greek wife.

The Ménagier de Paris (the Householder or Goodman of Paris, as we might say) wrote this book for the instruction of his young wife between 1392 and 1394. He was a wealthy man, not without learning and of great experience in affairs, obviously a member of that solid and enlightened *haute bourgeoisie*, upon which the French monarchy was coming to lean with ever-increasing confidence. When he wrote he must have been approaching old age, and he was certainly over sixty, but he had recently married a young wife of higher birth than himself, an orphan from a different province. He speaks several times of her "very great youth," and kept a sort of duenna-housekeeper with her to help and direct her in the management of his house; and indeed, like the wife of Isomachus, she was only fifteen years old when he married her. Modern opinion is shocked by a discrepancy in age between husband and wife, with which the Middle Ages, a time of *mariages de convenance*, was more familiar. "Seldom," the Ménagier says, "will you see ever so old a man who will not marry a young woman." Yet his attitude towards his young wife shows us that there may have been compensations, even in a marriage between May and January. Time after time in his book there sounds the note of a tenderness which is paternal rather than marital, a sympathetic understanding of the feelings of a wedded child, which a younger man might not have compassed. Over all the matter-of-fact counsels there seems to hang something of the mellow sadness of an autumn evening, when beauty and death go ever hand in hand. It was his wife's function to make comfortable his declining years; but it was his to make the task easy for her. He constantly repeats the assurance that he does not ask of her an overweening respect, or a service too humble or too hard, for such is not due to him; he desires only such care as his neighbours and kinswomen take of their husbands, "for to me belongeth none save the common service, or less."

In his Prologue, addressed to her, he gives a charming picture of the scene which led him to write his book: "You, being of the age of fifteen years and in the week that you and I were wed, did pray me that I would please to be indulgent to your youth and to your small and ignorant service mewards, until that you should have seen and learned more, to the hastening whereof you did promise me to set all care and diligence, . . . praying me humbly, in our bed as I remember, that for the love of God I would not correct you harshly before strangers nor before our own folk, but that I would correct you each night or from day to day in our chamber and show you the unseemly or foolish things done in the day or days past, and chastise you, if it pleased me, and then you would not fail to amend yourself according to my teaching and correction, and would do all in your power according to my will, as you said. And I thought well of, and praise and thank you for, what you said to me and I have often remembered it since. And know, dear sister,* that all that I know you have done since we were wed up to this day, and all that you shall do hereafter with good intent has been and is good and well hath pleased, pleases and shall please me. For your youth excuses you from being very wise, and will still excuse you in everything that you do with good intent to please me. And know that it doth not displease, but rather pleases me that you should have roses to grow and violets to care or and that you should make chaplets and dance and sing, and I would well that you should so continue among our friends and those of our estate, and it is but right and seemly thus to pass the time of your feminine youth, provided that you desire and offer not to go to the feasts and dances of too great lords, for that is not seemly for you, nor suitable to your estate nor mine." [1]

Meanwhile he has not forgotten her request that he would teach and correct her in private, and so he writes a little book (but it was a big book before he had finished) to show her how to comport herself; for he is sorry for this child, who has for long had neither father nor mother, and who is far from kinswomen who might counsel her, having "me only" he says, "for whom you have been taken from your kinsfolk and from the land of your birth." He has often deliberated the matter and now here is "an easy general introduction" to the whole art of being a wife, a housewife and a perfect lady. One characteristic reason, apart from his desire to help her and to be comfortable himself (for he was set in his ways), he gives for his trouble and recurs to from time to time, surely the strangest ever given by a husband for instructing his wife. He is old, he says, and must die before her, and it is positively essential that she should do him credit with her second husband. What a reflection upon him if she accompanied his successor to Mass with the collar of her *cotte* crumpled, or if she knew not how to keep fleas from the blankets, or how

* He addresses her throughout as "sister," a term of affectionate respect.

to order a supper for twelve in Lent! It is characteristic of
the Ménagier's reasonableness and solid sense that he regards
his young wife's second marriage with equanimity. One of his
sections is headed, "That you should be loving to your husband (whether myself or another), by the example of Sarah,
Rebecca, Rachel." How different from those husbands (dog-
in-the-manger, or anxious for the future of their children under a possibly harsh stepfather) whose wills so often reveal
them trying to bind their wives to perpetual celibacy after
their deaths, such husbands as William, Earl of Pembroke,
who died in 1469, admonishing his lady: "And wyfe, ye remember your promise to me to take the ordere of wydowhood,
as ye may be the better mastre of your owne to performe my
wylle."

The plan of the book "in three sections, containing nine-
teen principal articles," is most exhaustive. The first section
deals with religious and moral duties. In the words of the
Ménagier, "the first section is necessary to gain for you the
love of God and the salvation of your soul, and also to win
for you the love of your husband and to give you in this world
that peace which ought to be had in marriage. And because
these two things, to wit the salvation of your soul and the
comfort of your husband, are the two things most chiefly necessary, therefore are they here placed first." Then follows a
series of articles telling the lady how to say her morning
prayer when she rises, how to bear herself at Mass, and in
what form to make her confession to the priest, together with
a long and somewhat alarming discursus upon the seven
deadly sins, which it assuredly never entered into her sleek
little head to commit, and another on the corresponding virtues.[2] But the greater part of the section deals with the all-
important subject of the wife's duty to her husband. She is
to be loving, humble, obedient, careful and thoughtful for his
person, silent regarding his secrets, and patient if he be foolish
and allow his heart to stray towards other women. The whole
section is illustrated by a series of stories (known as *exempla*
in the Middle Ages), culled from the Bible, from the common
stock of anecdotes possessed by jongleur and preacher alike,

and (most interesting of all) from the Ménagier's own experience. Among the Ménagier's longer illustrations is the favourite but intolerably dull moral tale of Melibeu and Prudence, by Albertano of Brescia, translated into French by Renault de Louens, whose version the Ménagier copied, and adapted by Jean de Meung in the *Roman de la Rose*, from which in turn Chaucer took it to tell to the Canterbury Pilgrims. Here also are to be found Petrarch's famous tale of patient Griselda, which Chaucer also took and gave a wider fame, and a long poem written in 1342 by Jean Bruyant, a notary of the Châtelet at Paris, and called "The Way of Poverty and Wealth," inculcating diligence and prudence.[3]

The second section of the book deals with household management and is far the most interesting. The range of the Ménagier's knowledge leaves the reader gasping. The man is a perfect Mrs. Beeton! The section comprises a detailed treatise on gardening and another on the principles which should govern the engagement of servants and the method by which they should be managed when hired; the modern problem of servants who leave does not seem to have presented itself to him. There are instructions how to mend, air and clean dresses and furs, get out grease spots, catch fleas and keep flies out of the bedroom, look after wine and superintend the management of a farm.

At one point he breaks off, addressing his wife thus: "Here will I leave you to rest or to play and will speak no more to you; and while you disport yourself elsewhere I will speak to Master John, the Steward, who looks after our possessions, so that if there is anything wrong with any of our horses, whether for the plough or for riding, or if it is necessary to buy or exchange a horse, he may know a little of that it behoves him to know in this matter." There follow several pages of wise advice as to the good points of horses, how to examine them and to find their ages and defects under the eye of the horse dealer, the practical "tips" of a man who evidently knew and loved his horses, together with advice upon the treatment of their various diseases. Among the various recipes which the Ménagier gives to this intent are two charms; for instance, "when a horse has glanders, you must say to him these three words, with three paternosters: ✠ abgla, ✠ abgly, ✠ alphard, ✠ asy, ✠ pater noster, etc."[4]

Last, but not least, there is a magnificent cookery book, arranged in the form sacred to cookery books from that day to this, beginning with a list of specimen menus for dinners and suppers, hot or cold, fast or feast, summer or winter, giving hints on the choice of meat, poultry, and spices, and ending with a long series of recipes for all manner of soups, stews, sauces, and other viands, with an excursus on invalid's cookery!

The third section of the book was intended by the Ménagier to contain three parts: first of all, a number of parlour games for indoor amusement; secondly, a treatise on hawking, the favourite outdoor amusement of ladies; and thirdly, a list of amusing riddles and games of an arithmetical kind ("concerning counting and numbering, subtle to find out or guess"), presumably of the nature of our old friend, "If a herring and a half cost three ha'pence." Unfortunately, the Ménagier seems never to have finished the book, and of this section only the treatise on hawking has survived. It is a great pity, for we have several such treatises, and how interesting an account of indoor games and riddles might have been we may guess from a passage in the Ménagier's version of the story of Lucrece, when he describes the Roman ladies "some gossiping, others playing at *bric*, others at *qui féry*, others at *pince merille*, others at cards or other games of pleasure with their neighbours; others, who had supped together, were singing songs and telling fables and stories and wagers; others were in the street with their neighbours, playing at blind man's buff or at *bric* and at several other games of the kind."[5] In those days, before the invention of printing had made books plentiful, medieval ladies were largely dependent for amusement upon telling and listening to stories, asking riddles, and playing games, which we have long ago banished to the nursery; and a plentiful repertoire of such amusements was very desirable in a hostess. The Ménagier was clearly anxious that his wife should shine in the amenities as well as in the duties of social life.

Such was the monumental work which the Ménagier de Paris was able to present to his awed but admiring wife; and though it has been sadly neglected by historians it deserves to be well known, for it gives us a picture of a medieval housewife which it would be hard indeed to surpass. There is hardly a side of her daily life upon which it does not touch, and we may now with advantage look more closely upon her, and see in turn the perfect lady, whose deportment and manners do credit to her breeding; the perfect wife, whose submission to her husband is only equalled by her skill in ministering to his ease; the perfect mistress, whose servants love her and run her house like clockwork; and the perfect housewife, the Mrs. Beeton of the fifteenth century.

The Ménagier's views on deportment are incongruously sandwiched into his section on spiritual duties, under the general headings of getting up in the morning and going to church. His ideas on the subject of clothes are very clearly defined: a sweet disorder in the dress was in no way to his taste:

Know, dear sister, that if you wish to follow my advice you will have great care and regard for what you and I can afford to do, according to our estate. Have a care that you be honestly clad, without new devices and without too much or too little frippery. And before you leave your chamber and house, take care first that the collar of your shift, and of your *blanchet, cotte* and *surcotte*, do not hang out one over the other, as happens with certain drunken, foolish or witless women, who have no care for their honour, nor for the honesty of their estate or of their husbands, and who walk with roving eyes and head horribly reared up like a lion (*la teste espoventablement levée comme un lyon!*), their hair straggling out of their wimples, and the collars of their shifts and *cottes* crumpled the one upon the other, and who walk mannishly and bear themselves uncouthly before folk without shame. And if one speaks to them about it, they excuse themselves on the ground of their industry and humility, saying that they are so diligent, hardworking, and humble that they care not for themselves. But they lie; they care so much for themselves that if they were in an honourable company, never would they be willing that men should wait less upon them than upon the wiser ladies of like lineage with themselves, nor that they should have fewer salutations, bows, reverences and speech than the rest, but rather they desire more. And they are unworthy of it, for they know not how to maintain their own honourable fame, nay, nor the fame of their husbands and of their lineage, which they bring to shame. Therefore, fair sister, have a care that your hair, wimple, kerchief and hood and all the rest of your attire be well arranged and decently ordered, that none who see you can laugh or mock at you, but that all the others may find in you an example of fair and simple and decent array. . . . When you go to town or to church go suitably accompanied by honourable women according to your estate, and flee suspicious company, never allowing any ill famed woman to be seen in your presence. And as you go bear your head upright and your eyelids low and without fluttering, and look straight in front of you about four rods ahead, without looking round at any man or woman to the right or to the left, nor looking up, nor glancing from place to place, nor stopping to speak to anyone on the road.[6]

Such was the model of female deportment in the Middle Ages.

Let us pass from the lady to the wife. On the attitude of wife to husband the Ménagier's ideas are much the same as those of the rest of his age. They may be summed up as submission, obedience, and constant attention. She must be buxom at bed and at board, even in circumstances when buxomness hides a heavy heart. The good sense of the burgess does not prevent him from likening the wife's love for her husband to the fidelity of domestic animals towards their masters: "Of the domestic animals you see how a greyhound, or a mastiff, or a little dog, whether on the road, or at table, or in bed, always keeps near to the person from whom he takes his food, and leaves and is shy and fierce with all others; and

if the dog is afar off, he always has his heart and his eye upon
his master; even if his master whip him and throw stones
at him, the dog follows, wagging his tail and lying down
before his master, seeks to mollify him, and through rivers,
through woods, through thieves and through battles follows
him. . . . Wherefore for a better and stronger reason women,
to whom God has given natural sense and who are reasonable,
ought to have a perfect and solemn love for their husbands;
and so I pray you to be very loving and privy with your husband who shall be." [7] Patience is an essential quality in wives,
and, however sorely tried, they must never complain. The
Ménagier tells three stories to illustrate how a wife should
bear herself in order to win back the love of an unfaithful
husband. One of these is the famous tale of Griselda, but the
two others are drawn (so he says) from his own experience.
In the first of these he tells of the wife of a famous *avocat*
in the *parlement* of Paris, who saw to the nurture and marriage of her husband's illegitimate daughter; "nor did he ever
perceive it by one reproach, or one angry or ugly word." The
second is the charmingly told story of how John Quentin's
wife won back her husband's heart from the poor spinner of
wool to whom it had strayed.[8] All seem to show that the
Ménagier's simile of the little dog was selected with care,
for the medieval wife, like the dog, was expected to lick the
hand that smote her. Nevertheless, while subscribing to all
the usual standards of his age, the Ménagier's robust sense,
his hold upon the realities of life, kept him from pushing
them too far. The comment of another realist, Chaucer, on
the tale of Patient Griselda will be remembered. . . .

> Grisilde is deed and eek hire pacience,
> And bothe at ones buryed in Ytaille;
> For which I crie in open audience,
> No wedded man so hardy be t'assaille
> His wyves pacience in hope to fynde
> Grisildes, for in certein he shal faille!
>
> O noble wyves, ful of heigh prudence,
> Lat noon humylitee youre tonge naill,

Ne lat no clerk have cause or diligence
To write of yow a storie of swich mervaille
As of Grisildis pacient and kynde,
Lest Chichivache* yow swelwe in hire entraille! . . .

His creation of the Wife of Bath was an even more pointed
commentary. Here is what the Ménagier has to say to his
young wife on the same subject:

And I, who have put [the tale of Griselda] here only to
teach you, have not put it here to apply it to you, for I am
not worthy thereof, and I am not a marquis and I have not
taken you as a beggar, nor am I so foolish, so conceited or so
lacking in sense that I know not that 'tis not for me to assault
nor to assay you thus, nor in like manner. God keep me
from trying you thus under colour of false simulations. . . .
And forgive me that the story speaks (in my opinion) of too
great cruelty and beyond reason. And know that it never befel
so, but thus the tale runs and I may nor correct nor alter it,
for a wiser than I hath made it. And it is my desire that
since others have read it you also may know and be able to
talk about everything even as other folk do.[9]

Moreover, in spite of the ideal of submission which he
sets before his wife, the Ménagier has some charming words
to say about love—with a sigh, perhaps, for his own advanced
though not crabbed age, and a glance at that younger husband
of the future who shall one day enjoy his little bride.

In God's name (he says) I believe that when two good and
honourable people are wed, all other loves are put far off,
destroyed and forgotten, save only the love of each for the
other. And meseems that when they are in each other's presence, they look upon each other more than upon the others,
they clasp and hold each other and they do not willingly
speak or make sign save to each other. And when they are

* Chichevache, the lean cow who fed on patient wives, while
her mate Bicorne grew fat on humble husbands (A. W. Pollard).

separated, they think of each other and say in their hearts, "When I see him I shall do thus and thus to him, or say this to him, I shall beseech him concerning this or that." And all their special pleasure, their chief desire and their perfect joy is to do pleasure and obedience one to the other, if they love one another.[10]

The greater part of the Ménagier's book is concerned, however, not with the theoretical niceties of wifely submission, but with his creature comforts. His instructions as to how to make a husband comfortable positively palpitate with life; and at the same time there is something indescribably homely and touching about them; they tell more about the real life of a burgess's wife than a hundred tales of Patient Griselda or of Jehanne la Quentine. Consider this picture (how typical a product of the masculine imagination!) of the stout breadwinner, buffeted about in all weathers and amid all discomforts, nobly pursuing the task of earning his living, and fortified by the recollection of a domesticated little wife, darning his stockings at home by the fire, and prepared to lavish her attentions on the weary hero in the evening. The passage is an excellent example of the Ménagier's vivid and simple style, and of the use of incidents drawn from everyday life to illustrate his thesis, which is one of the chief charms of the book.

Fair sister, if you have another husband after me, know that you should think much of his comfort, for after a woman has lost her first husband she commonly finds it difficult to find another according to her estate, and she remains lonely and disconsolate for a long time;* and more so still, if she lose the second. Wherefore cherish the person of your husband carefully, and, I pray you, keep him in clean linen, for 'tis your business. And because the care of outside affairs lieth with men, so must a husband take heed, and go and come and journey hither and thither, in rain and wind, in snow and hail, now drenched, now dry, now sweating, now shivering,

---

* This seems to be contrary to experience.

ill-fed, ill-lodged, ill-warmed and ill-bedded; and nothing harms him, because he is upheld by the hope that he has of his wife's care of him on his return, and of the ease, the joys and the pleasures which she will do to him, or cause to be done to him in her presence; to have his shoes removed before a good fire, his feet washed and to have fresh shoes and stockings, to be given good food and drink, to be well served and well looked after, well bedded in white sheets and night-caps, well covered with good furs, and assuaged with other joys and amusements, privities, loves, and secrets, concerning which I am silent; and on the next day fresh shirts and garments. Certes, fair sister, such service maketh a man love and desire to return to his home and to see his goodwife and to be distant with other women.

And therefore I counsel you to make such cheer to your husband at all his comings and goings and to persevere therein; and also to be peaceable with him and remember the rustic proverb, which saith that there be three things which drive the goodman from home, to wit, a dripping roof, a smoking chimney and a scolding woman.[11] Wherefore, fair sister, I pray you that in order to keep yourself in love and good favour with your husband you be unto him gentle, amiable and debonair. Do unto him what the good simple women of our country say has been done unto their sons, when the lads have set their love elsewhere and their mothers cannot wean them from it. It is certain that when fathers and mothers be dead, and stepfathers and stepmothers argue with their stepsons, and scold them and repulse them, and take not thought for their sleeping, nor for their food and drink, their hose and their shirts and all their other needs and affairs, and the same children find elsewhere a good home and good counsel from some other woman, who receives them and takes thought to warm them with some poor gruel with her and to give them a bed and keep them tidy, mending their hosen, breeches, shirts and other garments, then those lads cleave to her and desire to be with her, and to sleep warm between her breasts, and are altogether estranged from their mothers and fathers, who before took no heed of them,

and now want to get them back and have them again. But
it may not be, for these children hold more dear the company
of strangers, who think and care for them, than that of their
kinsfolk, who have no care of them. Then the parents lament
and weep and say that these same women have bewitched
their children and that they are spellbound and cannot leave,
but are never easy save when they are with their enchantresses.
But whatever may be said of it, it is no witchcraft, but it is
by reason of the love, the care, the intimacies, joys and pleasures, which these women do in all ways unto the lads, and on
my soul there is no other enchantment. . . . Wherefore, dear
sister, I pray you thus to bewitch and bewitch again your husband, and beware of dripping roof and smoking fire, and scold
him not, but be unto him gentle and amiable and peaceable.
Be careful that in winter he has good fire without smoke, and
let him rest well and be well covered between your breasts
and thus bewitch him. . . . And thus you shall preserve and
guard him from all discomforts and give him all the ease that
you can, and serve him and cause him to be well served in
your house; and you shall look to him for outside things, for
if he be a good man he will take even more care and trouble
over them than you wish, and by doing as I have said, you
will make him always miss you and have his heart with you
and with your loving service, and he will shun all other houses,
all other women, all other services and households; all will
be naught to him save you alone, if you think of him as aforesaid. . . . And so on the road, husbands will think of their
wives, and no trouble will be a burden to them for the hope
and love they will have of their wives, whom they will long
to see, even as poor hermits, penitents and fasting monks
long to see the face of Christ Jesus; and husbands served
thus will never desire to abide elsewhere or in other company
but will withhold, withdraw and abstain themselves therefrom; all the rest will seem to them but a bed of stones
compared with their home.[12]

Enough has perhaps been quoted to show the Ménagier's
idea of a perfect wife; his idea of the perfect housewife is

contained in a mass of instructions which make excellently entertaining reading. So modern in tone is his section on the management of servants, both in his account of their ways and in his advice upon dealing with them, that one often rubs one's eyes to be sure that what one is reading is really a book written over five centuries ago by an old burgess of Paris. The Ménagier evidently had a fairly large household, and he probably owned a country as well as a town house, for he speaks several times of overseeing the farm-hands "when you are in the village." To assist his wife in superintending this large staff he has a *maître d'hôtel*, called Master John the Steward (*le despensier*), and a duenna, half housekeeper and half chaperon, for her young mistress, called Dame Agnes *la béguine*,* and a bailiff or foreman to look after the farm. The Ménagier divides his servants and workmen into three classes—first, those engaged by the day or by the season for special work, such as porters and carriers, reapers, winnowers, coopers, and so on; secondly, those engaged on piecework, such as tailors, furriers, bakers, and shoemakers, hired by medieval households of some wealth to make what was needed from raw material purchased at fairs or in the shops of the city; and thirdly, the ordinary domestic servants, who were hired by the year and lived in their master's house; "and of all these," he says, "there is none who does not gladly seek work and a master."

He gives an amusing account, evidently based upon bitter experience, of the wiles of the hired workman. He says that they are commonly lazy, rough, quick at "answering back," arrogant (except on payday) and ready to break into insults if unsatisfied with their pay. He warns his wife to bid Master John always to take the peaceable ones and always to bargain with them beforehand as to the pay for which they will do the work.

* The Béguines were a sort of religious order, or, more correctly, a lay sisterhood, standing half-way between the lay and the monastic life, and somewhat analogous to the Franciscan Tertiaries, or Third Order.

For know that most often they do not want to bargain, but they want to get to work without any bargain having been made and they say gently, "Milord, it is nothing—there is no need—you will pay me well and I shall be content with what you think fit." And if Master John take them thus, when the work is finished they will say, "Sir, there was more to do than I thought, there was this and that to do, and here and there," and they will not take what is given them and will break out into shouting and angry words . . . and will spread abroad evil report concerning you, which is worst of all.[13]

We know from the various ordinances fixing wages from the time of the Black Death onwards, that labour troubles were acute in France as well as in England at the end of the fourteenth century; and the Ménagier's advice throws an interesting sidelight on the situation.

It is, however, in his observations upon the engagement and management of maidservants that the wisdom of the serpent is most apparent. Incidentally he gives an account of how servants were hired in fourteenth-century Paris, which shows that the registry office and the character are by no means modern phenomena. There were *recommanderesses*—women holding what we should call registry offices—in Paris at this time, and an ordinance of 1351 (fixing wages after the Black Death) allows them to take 1s. 6d. for placing a chambermaid and 2s. for a nurse. A servant maid's wage at this time was 30s. a year and her shoes. The Ménagier counsels his wife thus on the delicate subject of interviewing and engaging her domestic chambermaids and serving men:

Know, dear sister (he says), that in order that they may obey you better and fear the more to anger you, I leave you the rule and authority to have them chosen by Dame Agnes the béguine, or by whichever other of your women you please, to receive them into our service, to hire them at your pleasure, to pay and keep them in our service as you please, and to dismiss them when you will. Nathless you should privily speak to me about it and act according to my advice, because you are too young and might be deceived by your own people. And know that of those chambermaids who are out of a place, many there be who offer themselves and clamour and seek urgently for masters and mistresses; and of these take none until you first know where their last place was, and send some of your people to get their character, to wit whether they talked or drank too much, how long they were in the place, what work they have been accustomed to doing and can do, whether they have homes or friends in the town, from what sort of people and what part of the country they come, how long they were there and why they left; and by their work in the past you shall find out what hope or expectation you may have of their work in the future. And know that ofttimes such women from distant parts of the country have been blamed for some fault in their own part of the world and that is what brings them into service at a distance. . . .

And if you find from the report of her master and mistress, neighbours and others that a girl is what you need, find out from her, and cause Master John to register in his account book, the day on which you engage her, her name and those of her father, mother and any of her kinsfolk, the place where they live and her birthplace and her references. For servants will be more afraid to do wrong if they know that you are recording all these things and that if they leave you without permission, or are guilty of any offence, you will write and complain to the justice of their country or to their friends. And notwithstanding bear in mind the saying of the philosopher called Bertrand the Old, who says that if you engage a maid or man of high and proud answers, you shall know that when she leaves she will miscall you if she can; and if, on the contrary, she be flattering and full of blandishments, trust her not, for she is in league with someone else to trick you; but if she blushes and is silent and shamefast when you correct her, love her as your daughter.[14]

The Ménagier's instructions as to how to look after servants when they have been engaged are equally practical. Good order is to be maintained, quarrels and bad language[15] prevented, and morals guarded. Each is to have his or her work assigned and to do it promptly. "If you order them to do something now and these your servants answer 'There is plenty of time, it shall be done,' or 'It shall be done to-morrow,' hold it as forgotten, it must all be begun again, it is as nought. And also when you give a general order to every one, each will wait for the other to do it, and it is the same." Not only is the work of the servants to be carefully super-intended by the mistress and by Dame Agnes, "who is with you," the Ménagier tells his wife, "in order to teach you wise and ripe behaviour and to serve and instruct you and to whom in particular I give the charge of this matter," but she is to show herself careful and benevolent in looking after their health and happiness. At the proper hour she is to cause them to sit down before a hearty meal of one sort of meat, avoiding rich viands, and one kind of drink, which must be nourish-ing but not intoxicating—"the cup that cheers but not inebriates"; probably in this case the light ale which was the habitual drink of the Middle Ages. She is to admonish them eat and drink their fill, but

as soon as they begin to tell stories, or to argue, or to lean on their elbows, order the béguine to make them rise and take away their table, for the common folk have a saying "when a varlet holds forth at table and a horse grazes in the ditch, it is time to take them away, for they have had their fill."

In the evening, after their afternoon's work, they are to have another hearty meal, and then in winter time they may warm themselves at the fire and take their ease. Then she is to lock up the house and pack them all off to bed.

And arrange first that each have beside his bed a candlestick in which to put his candle, and have them wisely taught to extinguish it with the mouth or hand before getting into bed and by no means with their shirts. And also have them admonished and taught each and all, that they must begin again the next day and that they must rise in the morning and each set to upon his own work.

The Ménagier further advises his wife that chambermaids

of fifteen to twenty years of age are foolish girls who do not know the world, and that she should always cause them to sleep near her in an antechamber, or a room without a skylight or a low window looking on to the street, and should make them get up and go to bed at the same time as herself. "And you yourself," he adds, "who, if God please, will be wise by this time, must keep them near to you." Moreover, if any of her servants fall ill, "do you yourself, laying aside all other cares, very lovingly and charitably care for him or her, and visit him and study diligently how to bring about his cure." [16]

But it is perhaps in his capacity as Mrs. Beeton that the Ménagier is most amusing. His infinite variety of household knowledge is shown in the incidental recipes which he gives when he is describing the measures which a wife must take for her lord's comfort, and the work of the servants. There are elaborate instructions concerning the costly medieval garments, worn year after year for a lifetime and often bequeathed in their owner's will, instructions for cleaning dresses and furs and for preserving them from moths, and instructions for removing stains and grease spots. The Ménagier gives seven recipes for taking out grease spots, but he is rather sceptical about one or two of them, which he has evidently copied from a book without trying them for himself. "To get rid of stains on a dress of silk, satin, camlet, damask cloth or another," runs one of these, "dip and wash the stain in verjuice and the stain will go; even if the dress be faded, it will regain its colour. *This I do not believe.*" The chief impression left, however, is that the medieval housewife was engaged in a constant warfare against fleas. One of the Ménagier's infallible rules for keeping a husband happy at home is to give him a good fire in the winter and keep his bed free from fleas in the summer. He gives six recipes for getting rid of such small livestock, which must indeed have been a very common trial to our forefathers:

In summer take heed that there be no fleas in your chamber nor in your bed, which you may do in six ways, as I have

heard tell. For I have heard from several persons that if the
room be scattered with alder leaves the fleas will get caught
therein. Item, I have heard tell that if you have at night
one or two trenchers of bread covered with birdlime or tur-
pentine and put about the room with a lighted candle set
in the midst of each trencher, they will come and get stuck
thereto. Another way which I have found and which is true:
take a rough cloth and spread it about your room and over
your bed and all the fleas who may hop onto it will be caught,
so that you can carry them out with the cloth wheresoever
you will. Item, sheepskins. Item, I have seen blankets placed
on the straw and on the bed and when the black fleas jumped
upon them they were the sooner found and killed upon the
white. But the best way is to guard oneself against those which
are within the coverlets and furs and the stuff of the dresses
wherewith one is covered. For know that I have tried this,
and when the coverlets, furs or dresses in which there be
fleas are folded and shut tightly up, in a chest straitly bound
with straps or in a bag well tied up and pressed, or otherwise
compressed so that the said fleas are without light and air and
kept imprisoned, then they will perish and die at once.[17]

A similar war had also to be waged against flies and mos-
quitoes, which rendered summer miserable. "I have sometimes," says the Ménagier, "seen in several chambers that
when one has gone to bed in them, they were full of mos-
quitoes, which at the smoke of the breath came to sit on the
faces of those who slept and sting them so that they were
fain to get up and light a fire of hay to smoke them off."
Against such pests he has also six infallible recipes—to wit,
a mosquito net over the bed; sprigs of fern hung up for the
flies to settle on; a bowl filled with a mixture of milk and
hare's gall, or with the juice of raw onions, which will kill
them; a bottle containing a rag dipped in honey, or else a
string dipped in honey to hang up; fly whisks to drive them
away; and closing up windows with oiled cloth or parch-
ment.[18]

The section on cookery, which contains the Ménagier's injunctions for "feeding the brute," is the longest in the book,

and gives an extraordinarily interesting picture of the domestic economy of our ancestors.[19] The Ménagier must have been brother to Chaucer's Franklin, "Epicurus owene sone":

> An housholdere, and that a greet, was he:
> Seint Julian he was in his contree;
> His breed, his ale, was alwey after oon;
> A bettre envyned man was nowher noon.
> Withoute bake mete was never his hous,
> Of fissh and flessh, and that so plenteuous
> It snewed in his hous of mete and drynke.
> Of alle deyntees that men koude thynke.
> After the sondry sesons of the yeer,
> So chaunged he his mete and his soper.
> Ful many a fat partrich had he in muwe
> And many a breem and many a luce in stuwe.
> Wo was his cook but if his sauce were
> Poynaunt and sharpe and redy al his geere.
> His table dormant in his hal alway
> Stood redy covered al the longe day.

In this, as in all other medieval cookery books, what strikes the modern reader is the length and elaboration of the huge feasts, with their many courses and dishes, and the richness of the highly spiced viands. There are black puddings and sausages, venison and beef, eels and herrings, fresh water fish, round sea fish and flat sea fish, common pottages unspiced, spiced pottages, meat pottages and meatless pottages, roasts and pastries and entremets, divers sauces boiled and unboiled, pottages and "slops" for invalids. Some of them sound delicious, others would be ruin to our degenerate digestions to-day. Pungent sauces of vinegar, verjuice, and wine were very much favoured, and cloves, cinnamon, galingale, pepper, and ginger appear unexpectedly in meat dishes. Almonds were a favourite ingredient in all sorts of dishes, as they still are in China and other parts of the East, and they might well be used more lavishly than they are in modern European cookery. True to his race, the Ménagier includes recipes for cooking frogs and snails.[20] To the modern cook some of his directions

may appear somewhat vague, as when he bids his cook to boil
something for as long as it takes to say a paternoster or a
miserere; yet for clockless kitchens in a pious age what clearer
indication could a man give? And, after all, it is no worse than
"cook in a hot oven," which still finds a place in many modern
cookery books which should know better. Other instructions
are detailed enough. In one valuable passage he gives a list of
all the meat markets of Paris, together with the number of
butchers to be found in each and the number of sheep, oxen,
pigs, and calves sold there every week, adding also for interest
the amount of meat and poultry consumed weekly in the
households of the King, the Queen and the royal children, the
Dukes of Orleans, Berry, Burgundy, and Bourbon. Elsewhere
also he speaks of other markets—the Pierre-au-Lait, or milk
market; the Place de Grève, where they sell coal and firewood;
and the Porte-de-Paris which is not only a meat market, but
the best place in which to buy fish and salt and green herbs
and branches to adorn your rooms.

For his wife's further guidance the Ménagier sets out a careful specification of the catering arrangements for several great
feasts—to wit, a dinner given by the Abbot of Lagny to the
Bishop of Paris and the members of the King's Council, the
feast, comprising dinner and supper, which one Master Elias
(evidently a grave and reverend *maître d'hôtel*, like Master
John *le despensier* himself) made for the wedding of Jean du
Chesne, upon a Tuesday in May, and the arrangements for
another wedding, "les nopces Hautecourt," in the month of
September, as to which the Ménagier observes "that because
they were widower and widow they were wed very early, in their
black robes and then put on others"; he was anxious that his
widow should do the correct thing at that second wedding of
hers. The description of the wedding feast arranged by Master
Elias is particularly detailed and valuable.[21] The careful
Ménagier, perhaps because he foresaw some big entertainment
which he must give to the burgesses and gentlemen of Paris,
perhaps because of his delightful interest in all the details of
material life, has set down at length not only the menu of the
dinner and supper, but a long account of the ingredients

needed, their quantities and prices, and the shops or markets where they must be bought, so that the reader can see with his eyes the *maître d'hôtel* and the cooks going round from stall to stall, visiting butcher and baker, poulterer, saucemaker, vintner, wafer maker, who sold the wafers and pastries dear to medieval ladies, and spicer whose shop was heavy with the scents of the East.

The Ménagier sets down also all the esquires and varlets and waiters who will be needed to serve such a feast as this. There was the master cook, comfortably stout and walking "high and disposedly," as Queen Elizabeth danced, brain pan stuffed full of delectable recipes, hand of ravishing lightness with pastries, eye and nose skilled to say when a capon was done to a turn, warranted without a rival

> To boille the chiknes with the marybones,
> And poudre-marchant tart and galyngale . . .
> He koude rooste and seethe and boille and frye,
> Maken martreux and wel bake a pye . . .
> For blankmanger, that made he with the beste.

He brought his varlets with him, and in Paris he took two francs for his hire "and perquisites" (a pregnant addition). Then there were ushers, "stout and strong," to keep the doors, and a clerk to add up the account; bread-cutters and water-carriers, two squires to serve at the dresser in the kitchen where the plates and dishes were handed out, two others at the hall dresser to give out spoons and drinking cups and pour wine for the guests, and two others in the pantry to give out the wine which their varlet kept drawing for them. There were the two *maîtres d'hôtel* to set out the silver salt-cellars for the high table, the four great gilded goblets, the four dozen hanaps, the four dozen silver spoons, the ewers and alms mugs and sweetmeat dishes, and to usher the guests to their places; a head waiter and two servitors for each table, a flower girl to make chaplets of flowers for the guests, women to see to the linen and deck the bridal bed,[22] and a washerwoman. The floors were strewn with violets and green herbs and the rooms decked with branches of May (all bought in the market in

early morning), and there was a good stock of torches and
candles, small candles to stand on the supper tables, and great
torches to be set in sconces on the walls, or to be carried in
procession by the guests, for the supper ended with "dancing,
singing, wine and spices and lighted torches." On this occasion
eight francs were given to the minstrels, over and above the
spoons and other presents made to them during the meal, and
there were also acrobats and mimes to amuse the guests. If they
had to prepare a great feast Master John and his little mistress
could not go far wrong after this, or fail to please the genial
epicure who set it down for them. The Ménagier copied many
of his recipes from other cookery books, but he must have got
the details of this entertainment from Master Elias himself,
and one can see their grey heads wagging with enjoyment, as
one talked and the other wrote.

The cookery book ends with a section containing recipes for
making what the Ménagier calls "small things which are not
necessities." There are various sorts of jams, mostly made
with honey; in the Middle Ages vegetables were evidently
much prepared in this way, for the Ménagier speaks of turnip,
carrot, and pumpkin jam. There is a delicious syrup of mixed
spices (at least the palate of faith must believe it to have been
delicious) and a powder of ginger, cinnamon, cloves, carda-
mom, and sugar, to be sifted over food, as sugar is sifted to-day;
there is a recipe for hippocras, and for "gauffres" or wafers,
and for candied oranges. There are various sage pieces of advice
as to the seasons for certain foods and the best ways of cooking
and serving them. Most amusing of all these are a number of
recipes not of a culinary nature—to wit, for making glue and
marking ink, for bringing up small birds in aviaries and cages,
preparing sand for hour-glasses, making rose-water, drying roses
to lay among dresses (as we lay lavender to-day), for curing
toothache, and for curing the bite of a mad dog. The latter is
a charm, of the same type as the Ménagier's horse charms:
"Take a crust of bread and write what follows: ✠ *Bestera*
✠ *bestie* ✠ *nay* ✠ *brigonay* ✠ *dictera* ✠ *sagragan* ✠ *es*
✠ *domina* ✠ *fiat* ✠ *fiat* ✠ *fiat* ✠ .'' Let us remember,

however, that the nation which produced it, some four centuries later produced Pasteur.

Enough has been said about this entrancing book to show how vividly it brings not only the Ménagier, but the Ménagier's young wife before our eyes after these many years. In the morning she rises, much earlier than ladies rise nowadays, though not so early as nuns, who must say matins, for that, her husband tells her, is not a fitting hour for married women to leave their beds. Then she washes, much less than ladies nowadays, hands and face only perchance, and says her orisons, and dresses very neatly, for she knows whose eye is upon her, and so goes with Dame Agnes the béguine to Mass, with eyes on the ground and hands folded over her painted primer. After Mass, and perhaps confession, back again to see if the servants are doing their work, and have swept and dusted the hall and the rooms, beaten the cushions and coverlets on the forms and tidied everything, and afterwards to interview Master John the steward and order dinner and supper. Then she sends Dame Agnes to see to the pet dogs and birds, "for they cannot speak and so you must speak and think for them if you have any." Then, if she be in her country house, she must take thought for the farm animals and Dame Agnes must superintend those who have charge of them, Robin the shepherd, Josson the oxherd, Arnoul the cowherd, Jehanneton the milkmaid, and Eudeline the farmer's wife who looks after the poultry yard. If she be in her town house she and her maids take out her dresses and furs from their great chests and spread them in the sun in the garden or courtyard to air, beating them with little rods, shaking them in the breeze, taking out spots and stains with one or other of the master's tried recipes, pouncing with lynx eyes upon the moth or sprightly flea.

After this comes dinner, the serious meal of the day, eaten by our ancestors about 10 a.m. What the Ménagier's wife gives to her lord and master will depend upon the time of year and upon whether it be a meat or a fast day; but we know that she has no lack of menus from which to choose. After dinner she sees that the servants are set to dine, and then the busy housewife may become the lady of leisure and amuse herself. If in the country she may ride out hawking with a gay party of neighbours; if in town, on a winter's day, she may romp and play with other married ladies of her tender years, exchange riddles or tell stories round the fire. But what she most loves is to wander in her garden, weaving herself garlands of flowers, violets, gilly flowers, roses, thyme, or rosemary, gathering fruit in season (she likes raspberries and cherries), and passing on to the gardeners' weighty advice about the planting of pumpkins ("in April water them courteously and transplant them"), to which the gardeners give as much attention as gardeners always have given, give still, and ever shall give, world without end, to the wishes of their employers. When she tires of this, the busy one gathers together Dame Agnes and her maids, and they sit under the carved beams of the hall mending his mastership's doublet, embroidering a vestment for the priest at his family chantry, or a tapestry hanging for the bed-chamber. Or perhaps they simply spin (since, in the words of the Wife of Bath, God has given women three talents—deceit, weeping, and spinning!); and all the while she awes them with that tale of Griselda, her voice rising and falling to the steady hum of the wheels.

At last it is evening, and back comes the lord and master. What a bustle and a pother this home-coming meant we know well, since we know what he expected. Such a running and fetching of bowls of warm water to wash his feet, and comfortable shoes to ease him; such a hanging on his words and admiring of his labours. Then comes supper, with a bevy of guests, or themselves all alone in the westering sunlight, while he smacks connoisseur's lips over the roast crane and the blank-manger, and she nibbles her sweet wafers. Afterwards an hour of twilight, when she tells him how she has passed the day, and asks him what she shall do with the silly young housemaid, whom she caught talking to the tailor's 'prentice through that low window which looks upon the road. There is warm affection in the look she turns up to him, her round little face puckered with anxiety over the housemaid, dimpling into a smile when he commends her; and there is warm affection and pride too in the look the old man turns down upon her. So the night falls, and they go round the house together, locking all the doors and seeing that the servants are safe abed, for our ancestors were more sparing of candlelight than we. And so to bed.

We may take our leave of the couple here. The Ménagier's wife evidently had a full life.

> Some respit to husbands the weather may send,
> But huswiues affaires haue neuer an end.

There was no room in it for the idleness of those lovely ladies, with their long fingers, whom Langland admonished to sew for the poor. Moreover, exaggerated as some of her husband's ideas upon wifely submission appear to-day, the book leaves a strong impression of good sense and of respect as well as love for her. The Ménagier does not want his wife to be on a pedestal, like the troubadour's lady, nor licking his shoes like Griselda; he wants a helpmeet, for, as Chaucer said, "If that wommen were nat goode and hir counseils goode and profitable, oure Lord God of hevene wolde never han wroght hem, ne called hem 'help' of man, but rather confusioun of man." [23] Ecclesiastical Jeremiahs were often wont to use the characteristically medieval argument that if God had meant woman for a position of superiority He would have taken her from Adam's head rather than his side; but the Ménagier would have agreed with the more logical Peter Lombard, who observed that she was not taken from Adam's head, because she was not intended to be his ruler, nor from his feet either, because she was not intended to be his slave, but from his side, precisely, because she was intended to be his companion. There is something of this spirit in the Ménagier's attitude towards his little wife, and it is this which makes his book so charming and causes it to stand head and shoulders above most other medieval books of behaviour for women. But, above all, its social and historical value lies in the fact that it gives us, in hues undimmed by time, a full length portrait of a medieval housewife, who has her place (and it is a large one) in history, but concerning whom historians have almost invariably been silent.

CHAPTER V

THOMAS BETSON

A Merchant of the Staple in the Fifteenth Century

Some men of noble stock were made, some glory in the murder
    blade;
Some praise a Science or an Art, but I like honourable Trade!
          —JAMES ELROY FLECKER,
               The Golden Journey to Samarcand

THE visitor to the House of Lords, looking respectfully upon
that august assembly, cannot fail to be struck by a stout and
ungainly object facing the throne—an ungainly object upon
which in full session of Parliament, he will observe seated the
Lord Chancellor of England. The object is a woolsack, and it
is stuffed as full of pure history as the office of Lord Chancellor
itself. For it reminds a cotton-spinning, iron-working generation that the greatness of England was built up, not upon the
flimsy plant which comes to her to be manufactured from the
Far East and West of the world, nor upon the harsh metal
delved from her bowels, but upon the wool which generation
after generation has grown on the backs of her black-faced
sheep. First in the form of a raw material sought after ea-
gerly by all the cloth-makers of Europe, then in the form of a
manufacture carried on in her own towns and villages, and sent
out far and wide in ships, wool was the foundation of England's
greatness right up to the time of the Industrial Revolution,
when cotton and iron took its place. So if you look at old
pictures of the House of Lords, in Henry VIII's reign, or in
Elizabeth's, you will see the woolsack before the throne,[1] as
you will see it if you visit the House to-day. The Lord Chancellor of England is seated upon a woolsack because it was
upon a woolsack that this fair land rose to prosperity.
  The most remarkable body of traders in England during the

Middle Ages were the Merchants of the Staple, who traded
in wool. The wool trade had for long been the largest and most
lucrative body of trade in the country, and it was one in which
the Kings of England were particularly interested, for their
customs revenue was drawn largely from wool and wool fells;
and, moreover, when they desired to borrow money in anticipation of revenue it was to the wool merchants that they
turned, because the wool merchants were the wealthiest traders in the country. For these and other reasons the Government adopted the custom of fixing staple towns, which acted
as centres of distribution through which the export trade was
forced to go. The location of the Staple was altered from time
to time; sometimes it was at Bruges, sometimes at Antwerp,
sometimes in England; but usually it was at Calais,
where it was first fixed in 1363 and finally established in 1423.
Through the Staple all wool and wool fells, hides, leather, and
tin had to pass, and the organization of the system was complete when the body of wool merchants, in whose hands lay
the bulk of the Staple trade, were finally incorporated in 1354,
under the governance of a mayor. The system was a convenient
one for Crown and merchants alike. The Crown could
concentrate its customs officers in one place and collect its
customs the more easily, particularly as a method was gradually
developed by which the custom and subsidy on wool was paid
to the Royal officials by the Fellowship of the Staple, who then
collected it from the individual members. The merchants, on
the other hand, benefited by the concentration in trade: they
were able to travel in groups and to organize convoys to protect
the wool fleets from pirates who swarmed in the narrow seas
between England and France; as members of a powerful cor-
poration they could secure both privileges and protection in
Flanders. Moreover, the wool buyers also benefited by the
arrangement, which rendered possible a careful surveillance by
the Crown and the Company of the Staple of the quality of
the wool offered for sale, and a series of regulations against
fraud. It must be remembered that in days when trade stood
in need of a protection which the Government was not yet able
to give it, there was nothing unpopular in the idea of giving

the monopoly of the staple trade to the members of a single company. "Trade in companies is natural to Englishmen," wrote Bacon; and for four centuries it was the great trading companies which nurtured English trade and made this country the commercial leader of the world.

The wool trade throve in England until the close of the Middle Ages, but throughout the fifteenth century the staplers were beginning to feel the competition of another company— that of the famous Merchant Adventurers, who, taking advantage of the growth in the native cloth manufacture during the previous century, had begun to do a great trade in the export of cloth. This was obnoxious to the staplers, who desired the continuance of the old system, by which they exported English wool to the Continent, where at Ypres and Ghent, Bruges and Mechlin, and the other famous cloth-working cities of the Netherlands, it was woven into fine cloth. This cloth manufacture gave to the Netherlands a sort of industrial pre-eminence in Europe throughout the Middle Ages, and it was dependent entirely upon a good supply of English wool, for the next best wool in Europe—that of Spain—was not satisfactory unless mixed with wool of English growth. Hence the close political tie between England and Flanders, the one needing a customer, the other an essential raw material; for, as a fifteenth century poet said,

the lytelle londe of Flaundres is
But a staple to other londes, iwys,
And alle that groweth in Flaundres, greyn and sede,
May not a moneth fynde hem mete and brede.
What hath thennc Flaundres, be Flemmyngis leffe or lothe
But a lytelle madcre and Flemmyshe clothe?
By drapynge of our wolle in substaunce
Lyvene here comons, this is here governaunce;
Wythought whyche they may not leve at ease,
Thus moste hem sterve, or wyth us most have peasse.[2]

In those days the coat on the Englishman's back was made out of English wool, indeed, but it had been manufactured in Flanders, and the staplers saw no reason why it should ever be otherwise. As to the Flemings, the political alliances which commercial necessities constantly entailed between the two countries gave rise among them to a proverb that they bought the fox-skin from the English for a groat and sold them back the tail for a guelder;[3] but it was the sheepskin which they bought, and they were not destined to go on buying it for ever. The great cloth-making cities of the Netherlands were finally ruined by the growth of the English cloth manufacture, which absorbed the English wool. However, in spite of the growing prosperity of this trade, which had by the beginning of the sixteenth century ousted that of wool as the chief English export trade, the Company of the Merchants of the Staple was still great and famous throughout the fifteenth century.

Many were the wealthy and respected staplers who were in those days to be found directing the destinies of English towns, mayors of London and provincial ports, contractors and money-lenders to an impecunious king, so rich and so powerful that they became a constitutional menace, almost, it has been said, a fourth estate of the realm, with which His Majesty was wont to treat for grants apart from Parliament. Many are the staplers' wills preserved in registries up and down England and bearing witness to their prosperity and public spirit. Many are the magnificent brasses which preserve their memory in the parish churches of the Cotswolds and other wool-growing districts of England. At Chipping Campden lies William Grevel with his wife, "late citizen of London and flower of the wool merchants of all England," who died in 1401, and his beautiful house still stands in the village street. At Northleach lies John Fortey, who rebuilt the nave before he died in 1458; his brass shows him with one foot on a sheep and the other on a woolpack, and the brasses of Thomas Fortey, "woolman," and of another unknown merchant, with a woolpack, lie near by. At Linwood, at Cirencester, at Chipping Norton, at Lechlade, and at All Hallows, Barking, you may see others of the great fraternity.[4] They rest in peace now, but when they lived they were the shrewdest traders of their day. Of wool, cries the poet Gower,

O leine, dame de noblesce
Tu est des marchantz la duesse,
Pour toy servir tout sont enclin—

"O wool, noble dame, thou art the goddess of merchants, to serve thee they are all ready; by thy good fortune and thy wealth thou makest some mount high, and others thou bringest to ruin. The staple where thou dwellest is never free of fraud and trickery, wherewith man wounds his conscience. O wool, Christians no less than pagans and Saracens seek to have thee and confess thee. O wool, we should not be silent about thy doings in strange lands; for the merchants of all countries, in time of peace, in time of war, come to seek thee by reason of their great love, for whoever else hath enemies thou art never without good friends, who have given themselves to thy profitable service. Thou art cherished throughout the world, and the land where thou art born may do great things by reason of thee. Thou art carried throughout the world by land and sea, but thou goest to the wealthiest men; in England art thou born, but it is said that thou art but ill governed, for Trick, who hath much money, is made regent of thy staple; at his will he taketh it to foreign lands, where he purchaseth his own gain to our harm. O fair, O white, O delightful one, the love of thee stings and binds, so that the hearts of those who make merchandise of thee cannot escape. So they compass much trickery and many schemes how they may gather thee, and then they make thee pass the sea, queen and lady of their navy, and in order to have thee envy and covetousness hie them to bargain for thee." [5]

The daily life of a Merchant of the Staple is not a difficult one to reconstruct, partly because the Golden Fleece has left so many marks upon our national life, partly because the statute book is full of regulations concerning the wool trade, but chiefly because there have come down to us many private letters from persons engaged in shipping wool from England to Calais. Of all the different sorts of raw material out of which the history of ordinary people in the Middle Ages has to be made, their letters are perhaps the most enthralling, be-

cause in their letters people live and explain themselves in all
their individuality. In the fifteenth century most men and
women of the upper and middle classes could read and write,
although their spelling was sometimes marvellous to behold,
and St. Olave's Church is apt to become "Sent Tolowys
scryssche" beneath their painfully labouring goose quills, and
punctuation is almost entirely to seek. But what matter? their
meaning is clear enough. Good fortune has preserved in various
English archives several great collections of family letters
written in the fifteenth century. Finest of all are the famous
Paston Letters, written by and to a family of Norfolk gentle-
folk, and crammed with information about high politics and
daily life.[6] Less interesting, but valuable all the same, are the
letters of the Plumptons, who were lords in Yorkshire.[7] But
for our purposes the most interesting are two other collections,
to wit, the correspondence of the Stonors, whose estates lay
chiefly in Oxfordshire and the neighbouring counties; and the
Cely papers, kept by a family of Merchants of the Staple.

These two collections give us a vivid picture of wool staplers
in their public and private lives. The Cely papers cover the
years 1475 to 1488, and it so happens that during that period
William Stonor (he became Sir William in 1478) also became
interested in the wool trade, for in 1475 he married Elizabeth
Riche, the daughter and widow of wealthy city merchants. The
Stonors had great sheep runs on their estates in the Chilterns
and Cotswolds, and William readily perceived the advantage
of his alliance with Elizabeth's family, who were interested in
the wool trade. Consequently he entered into a partnership
with a friend of his wife's, a Merchant of the Staple in Calais,
named Thomas Betson, who is the subject of this study, and
until Elizabeth's death in 1479, he took an active part in the
export trade. Thomas Betson died in 1486, and was thus an
exact contemporary of those other Merchants of the Staple,
George and Richard Cely, whom he must have known; indeed,
William Cely, their cousin and agent, writes from London to
George in Calais in 1481, advising him that he has dispatched
464 fells to him in the "Thomas" of Newhithe, "and the sayd
felles lyeth nexte be afte the maste lowest under the felles of

Thomas Bettson." [8] By the aid of the "Stonor Letters and Papers," which contain many letters from and concerning him during the years of his partnership with Sir William, and of the "Cely Papers," which are full of information about the life of a Merchant of the Staple at Calais, Thomas Betson may be summoned before us by a kindly magic until he almost lives again. So he deserves to do, for he is one of the most delightful people revealed to us in any of the fifteenth-century letters; for honest charm he has no rival save the attractive Margery Brews, who married John Paston the younger, and shows up so pleasantly beside the hard Paston women.

Perhaps the reason why our hearts warm immediately towards Thomas Betson is that our first meeting with him plunges us immediately into a love affair. His first letter to William Stonor is dated April 12, 1476, and informs William that their wool has come in to Calais. "Right worshipfful Syr," it begins, "I recomaund me unto your good maystershipe, and to my right worshipffulle maystresse your wiffe, and yf it plese your maystershipe, to my maystresse Kateryn." [9] Ten days later he writes again from London, on the eve of sailing for Calais, thanking Stonor for his "gentle cheer and faithful love, the which alway ye bear and owe unto me, and of my behalf nothing deserved," * announcing that he has sent a present of powdered † lampreys from himself and a pipe of red wine from his brother, and adding this postscript: "Sir, I beseech your mastership that this poor writing may have me lowly recommended to my right worshipful mistress, your wife, and in like wise to my gentle cousin and kind mistress Katherine Riche, to whom I beseech your mastership ever to be favourable and loving." [10] Who was this Katherine Riche to whom he so carefully commends himself? Katherine Riche was William Stonor's step-daughter, one of his wife's children by her first husband; she was Thomas Betson's affianced bride, and at this time she was about thirteen years old.

Modern opinion, which is happily in favour of falling in

* Henceforth I shall modernize spelling, for the reader's convenience.
† I.e. pickled.

love, and of adult marriages, is often shocked by the air of business which pervades matchmaking in the days of chivalry, and by the many cases of grown men married to little girls not yet out of their teens. In those days it was held that a boy came of age at fourteen and a girl at twelve (a discrepancy which the great canon lawyer, Lyndwood, the son of a stapler,[11] attributed to the fact that ill weeds grow apace!). For reasons of property, or to settle family feuds, or simply to assure their own future, babies in cradles were sometimes betrothed and even married; all that the Church required was that children should be free when they came of age (at the ages of fourteen and twelve!) to repudiate the contract if they so desired. Nothing seems to separate modern England from the good old days so plainly as the case of little Grace de Saleby, aged four, who for the sake of her broad acres was married to a great noble, and on his death two years later to another, and yet again, when she was eleven, to a third, who paid three hundred marks down for her.[12] There is an odd mixture of humour and pathos in the story of some of these marriages. John Rigmarden, aged three, was carried to church in the arms of a priest, who coaxed him to repeat the words of matrimony, but halfway through the service the child declared that he would learn no more that day, and the priest answered, "You must speak a little more, and then go play you." James Ballard, aged ten, was married to Jane his wife "at x of the clocke in the night without the consent of any of his frendes, bie one Sir Roger Blakey, then curate of Colne and the morowe after, the same James declarid vnto his Vnckle that the said Jane [beyinge a bigge damsell and mariageable at the same tyme] had intised him with two Apples, to go with her to Colne and to marry her." Elizabeth Bridge *née* Ramsbotham, says that after her marriage to John Bridge, when he was eleven and she thirteen, he never used her "lovinglie, insomoche that the first night they were maried, the said John wold Eate no meate at supper, and whan hit was bed tyme, the said John did wepe to go home with his father, he beynge at that tyme at her brother's house." [13]

Sometimes, however, medieval records throw a pleasanter

light on these child marriages. Such was the light thrown by the Ménagier de Paris's book for his young wife, so kindly, so affectionate, so full of indulgence for her youth; and such also is the light thrown by the charming letter which Thomas Betson wrote to little Katherine Riche on the first day of June in 1476. It is a veritable gem, and it is strange that it has not attracted more notice, for certainly no anthology of English letters should be without it. I set it down here at length, for it brings to warm life again both Thomas Betson and Katherine Riche:

Mine own heartily beloved Cousin Katherine, I recommend me unto you with all the inwardness of my heart. And now lately ye shall understand that I received a token from you, the which was and is to me right heartily welcome, and with glad will I received it; and over that I had a letter from Holake, your gentle squire, by the which I understand right well that ye be in good health of body, and merry at heart. And I pray God heartily in his pleasure to continue the same: for it is to me very great comfort that he so be, so help me Jesu. And if ye would be a good eater of your meat alway, that ye might wax and grow fast to be a woman, ye should make me the gladdest man of the world, by my troth; for when I remember your favour and your sad loving dealing to me wards, for sooth ye make me even very glad and joyous in my heart; and on the tother side again, when I remember your young youth, and see well that ye be none eater of your meat, the which should help you greatly in waxing, for sooth then ye make me very heavy again. And therefore I pray you, mine own sweet Cousin, even as you love me, to be merry and eat your meat like a woman. And if ye will so do for my love, look what ye will desire of me, whatsoever it be, and by my troth, I promise you by the help of our Lord to perform it to my power. I can no more say now, but on my coming home I will tell you much more between you and me and God before. And whereas ye, full womanly and like a lover, remember me with manifold recommendation in divers manners, remitting the same to my discretion to depart them there as I love best, for sooth, mine own sweet Cousin, ye shall understand that with good heart and good will I receive and take to myself the one half of them and them will I keep by me; and the tother half with hearty love and favour I send them to you, mine own sweet Cousin, again, for to keep by you; and over that I send you the blessing that our Lady gave her dear son, and ever well to fare. I pray you greet well my horse and pray him to give you four of his years to help you withal; and I will at my coming home give him four of my years and four horse loaves till amends. Tell him that I prayed him so. And Cousin Katherine, I thank you for him, and my wife shall thank you for him hereafter; for ye do great cost upon him, as is told me. Mine own sweet Cousin, it was told me but late that ye were at Calais* to seek me, but could not see me nor find me; forsooth ye might have comen to my counter, and there ye should both find me and see me, and not have faulted of me; but ye sought me in a wrong Calais, and that ye should well know if ye were here and saw this Calais, as would God ye were and some of them with you that were with you at your gentle Calais. I pray you, gentle Cousin, commend me to the clock, and pray him to amend his unthrifty manners; for he strikes ever in undue time, and he will be ever afore, and that is a shrewd condition. Tell him without he amend his condition that he will cause strangers to avoid and come no more there. I trust to you that he shall amend against mine coming, the which shall be shortly, with all hands and all feet, with God's grace. My very faithful Cousin, I trust to you that though all I have not remembered my right worshipful mistress your mother afore in this letter, that ye will of your gentleness recommend me to her mistresship as many times as it shall please you: and ye may say, if it please you, that in Whitsun week next I entend to the mart ward. And I trust you will pray for me; for I shall pray for you and, so it may be, none so well. And Almighty Jesu make you a good woman and send you many good years and long to live in health and virtue to his pleasure. At great Calais, on this side on the sea, the first day of June, when every man was

* Possibly an inn with that name (?).

gone to his dinner, and the clock smote nine, and all your
household cried after me and bade me "Come down, come
down to dinner at once!"—and what answer I gave them, ye
know it of old.

By your faithful Cousin and lover Thomas Betson. I send you
this ring for a token.

So ending, Thomas Betson smiled, dropped a kiss on the seal
and inscribed his letter, "To my faithful and heartily beloved cousin Katherine Riche at Stonor, this letter be delivered in haste." [14]

Henceforth there begins a charming triangular correspondence between Betson and Stonor and Dame Elizabeth Stonor,
in which family news and business negotiations are pleasantly
mingled. Dame Elizabeth and Betson were on the best of
terms, for they had been old friends before her second marriage. A special chamber was kept for him at Stonor, and by an
affectionate anticipation she often refers to him as "My son
Betson." Almost all her letters to her husband contain news of
him—how he took his barge at 8 a.m. in the morning and God
speed him, how no writing has come from him these eight
days, how he has now written about the price to be paid for
forty sacks of Cotswold wool, how he recommends him to Sir
William and came home last Monday. Sometimes he is entrusted with the delicate business of interviewing Dame Elizabeth's mother, a difficult old lady with a tongue; "God send
her," says Thomas, mopping his brow, after one of these
interviews, "once a merry countenance or shortly to the
Minories!" * After another he writes to Dame Elizabeth: "Sith
I came home to London I met with my lady your mother and
God wot she made me right sullen cheer with her countenance
whiles I was with her; methought it long till I was departed.
She break out to me of her old 'ffernyeres' and specially she
brake to me of the tale I told her between the vicar that was
and her; she said the vicar never fared well sith, he took it so

* The convent of Minoresses, or Franciscan nuns, outside
Aldgate.

much to heart. I told her a light answer again and so I departed from her. I had no joy to tarry with her. She is a fine merry woman, but ye shall not know it nor yet find it, nor none of yours by that I see in her." [15] It was the faithful Betson, too, who was chosen to look after his Katherine's little sister Anne when she was ill in London, and he writes home asking for her clothes—"She hath need unto them and that knoweth our Lord"—and complaining of the old grandmother's behaviour: "If my lady your mother meet my cousin Anne she will say no more but 'God's blessing have ye and mine,' and so go her way forth, as though she had no joy of her." [16] It was Betson, too, who escorted Dame Elizabeth, when need was, from Windsor to London and wrote to her husband: "By the way we were right merry, thanked be God, and so with his mercy we mean here to be merry for the season that my lady is here, and when your mastership is ready to come hitherwards, we here shall so welcome you that the season of your abiding shall not be noisome, with God's grace." [17] Whereupon Sir William sends a present of capons by the carrier to assist the merriment, and Betson reports, "Sir, I took two capons, but they were not the best, as ye counselled me by your letter to take, and indeed to say the truth I could not be suffered. My lady your wife is reasonably strong waxed, the Lord be thanked, and she took her will in that matter like as she doth in all other." [18]

There are, indeed, a hundred evidences of the warmth of Betson's affection for the Stonors and of the simple piety of his character. Sometimes he ventures to give them good advice. Dame Elizabeth was somewhat uplifted by her elevation from the ranks of the mercantile bourgeoisie to a place among the country gentry, and was apt to be extravagant, nor was her husband entirely guiltless of running up bills. We hear of the ale brewer and the bread baker calling daily upon his agent for money, and on one occasion the Stonors owed over £12 to Betson's own brother, a vintner, for various pipes of red and white wine and a butt of Rumney.* [19] So Thomas writes to Dame Elizabeth, on his way to the mart: "Our blessed lord Jesus

* Greek wine.

Christ preserve you both in honour and worship virtuously to continue in God's pleasure and also to send you good and profitable counsel and grace to do hereafter. This is and shall be my prayer forsooth every day; your honour and worship of countenance hereafter sticketh as nigh mine heart as doth any friend, man or other about you, by my troth, our blessed Lord so help me. I will avise you, Madam, to remember large expenses and beware of them, and in likewise my master your husband; it is well done ye remember him of them, for divers considerations, as ye know both right well. And our blessed Lord be your comforter and help in all your good work. Amen." [20] A month later he hears that William Stonor has been ill and writes to sympathize with Dame Elizabeth: "And if I could do anything here that might be to his pleasure and yours, I would I knew it and it should be done withouten fail. Truly your discomfort is not my comfort, God knoweth it. Nevertheless your ladyship must cause him to be merry and of glad cheer, and to put away all fantasies and unthrifty thoughts, that comes no good of, but only hurtful. A man may hurt himself by riotous means; it is good to beware." [21]

Meanwhile what of little Katherine Riche? She recurs over and over in Thomas Betson's letters. Occasionally she is in disgrace, for she was not handy with her pen. "I am wroth with Katherine," writes he to her mother, "because she sendeth me no writing. I have to her divers times and for lack of answer I wax weary; she might get a secretary if she would and if she will not, it shall put me to less labour to answer her letters again." [22] But the important thing is that she grows steadily older, though not quickly enough to please our lover. On Trinity Sunday in 1478 he writes to Dame Elizabeth: "I remember her full oft, God know[eth] it. I dreamed once she was thirty winters of age and when I woke I wished she had been but twenty and so by likelihood I am sooner like to have my wish than my dream, the which I beseech Almighty Jesu heartily when it shall please Him" [23]; and to the lady's stepfather he writes a month later: "I beseech you to remember my cousin Katherine. I would she did well, God knoweth it, and ye deme, as I trow, if I had found her at

home here my comfort should have been the more; but I
thank God of all. My pain is the more; I must needs suffer as I
have done in times past, and so will I do for God's sake and
hers." [24] However, Katherine was now fifteen years of age and
was sufficiently grown up to wed, and the next letter, written
a week later to Dame Elizabeth, shows us Thomas Betson beginning to set his house in order and getting exceedingly
bothered about laying in her trousseau, a business with which
Dame Elizabeth had, it seems, entrusted the future bridegroom.

Madam, and it like you, I understand by your writing that
it will be the latter end of August or your ladyship can come
here to London; and if it should be so I would be sorry, for I
have much to do and I can little skill to do anything that
longeth to the matter ye wot of [evidently the preparations
for Katherine] . . . I must beseech your ladyship to send me
[your advice] how I shall be demeaned in such things as shall
belong unto my cousin Katherine, and how I shall provide for
them. She must have girdles, three at the least, and how they
shall be made I know not, and many other things she must
have, ye know well what they be, in faith I know not; by my
troth, I would it were done, liever than more than it shall
cost. . . . And as for the sending hither of my Cousin Katherine, your ladyship may do therein as it shall please you. I
would she knew as much as you know, forsooth, and then she
should do some good and help me in many things when she
come. . . . Also, madam, as ye write me the courteous dealing of my master with my Cousin Katherine, etc., truly I am
very glad thereof and I pray God heartily thank him therefore,
for he hath ever been lovingly disposed [unto] her, and so I
beseech God ever continue him and also my Cousin Katherine to deserve it unto him by her goodly demeanour and womanly disposition, as she can do right well if her list, and so saith
every body that praiseth her.[25]

The note of pride in the last words is as engaging as the im-
patience of the harassed male faced with the choosing of
girdles. Even more charming is the letter which he wrote the

same day to Sir William Stonor. He is a little incoherent with joy and gratitude, full of regrets that business keeps him from Stonor and good wishes for the health of the family. "I fare like a sorry piper," he says. "When I begin I cannot leave, but yet once again our blessed Lord be your speed and your help." Of Katherine he writes thus:

I understand by the worshipful report of your mastership the [be]haviours of my cousin Katherine unto you, to my lady your wife and to all other, etc.; and truly it is to me right joyful and comfortable gladness to hear of her and I beseech our blessed Lord ever to preserve her in all virtue and good living to his pleasure, and to reward your mastership with heaven at your ending, for your good disposition to herwards in good exhortations giving. And that I wot well of old, or else truly she could not be of that disposition, virtuous and goodly, her youth remembered and excused. . . . Sir, remember your mastership well what ye have written of my Cousin Katherine; truly I shall when I speak with her, tell her every word, and if I find the contrary. Our vicar here, so God help me, shall cry out upon her* within this ten weeks and less, and by that time I shall be ready in every point, by God's grace, and so I would she were, forsooth ye may believe me of it.[26]

This letter was written on June 24, 1478, and Thomas probably married his little Katherine in August or September, for when Dame Elizabeth writes to her husband on October 5th, she says, "My son Betson and his wife recommend them to you." [27] The poor child was to learn soon enough some of the sorrows of a wife, for a year later Thomas Betson fell dangerously ill, and she was nursing him and looking after his business for all the world as though she were a grave matron and not a bride of sixteen. Moreover, she must already have been expecting the birth of her eldest son. William Stonor's attitude towards his partner's illness is not without humour. He was torn between anxiety for the life of a friend and an even greater anxiety that Betson should not die without setting

* I.e. call the banns.

straight the business obligations between them. We hear of the
illness and of Katherine's labours in a letter from one of
Stonor's agents to his master:

Sir, according to the commandment of your mastership,
we were at Stepney by nine of the clock; at such time as we
came thither we saw the gentleman forthwith, and in good
faith he made us good cheer as a sick man might by countenance notwithstanding, for in good faith we saw by his demeanour that he might not prosper in this world, for Mistress
Bevice and other gentlewomen and his uncle were of the
same opinion. And we desired and prayed him to be of good
comfort and so comforted him as heartily as we could in your
name and in my lady's, and so we departed from the chamber down into the hall, and he fell into a great slumbering and
was busily moved in his spirits. And at eleven of the clock I
called his uncle out of his bed into the gentleman's chamber,
and I asked his advice and my mistress his wife, of the stock
and of the demeanour thereof for the year and the half that is
last past. And touching the stock he confessed that it was
£1,160, wherein at the sight of your acquittance in discharging
of him and all his doers that shall be behind him, the said
stock shall be ready. And as for the occupation of it, as he will
answer between God and devil, the book that he bought it by
ye shall be privy thereto; and the book that he sold by ye shall
be also privy to, which two books shall be his judges, which
remain in the keeping of my mistress his wife's hands under
lock and key and other bills and obligations according, concerning the surety for divers payments to be made to divers
merchants, as the said lord saith. . . . And as for the plate my
mistress Jane [probably Jane Riche, the younger sister of Kath-
erine] and I have caused it to be taken up and set in surety,
save that that must needs be occupied.

He sends to Sir William for information about two sums of
£80 each owed by Betson to his master and mistress, and adds:

I trust to Jesu he shall endure till the messenger come
again; longer the physicians have not determined. The execu-

tors be three persons, my mistress his wife, Humphrey Starkey, Recorder of London, Robert Tate, merchant of Calais; notwithstanding I moved him, between him and me and mistress Jane, that he should break this testament and make my mistress his wife sole executrix. What will be done therein as yet I cannot speak, but I shall do as I can, with God's grace.[28]

There is something unexpected and a little vulture-like about this gathering of creditors and seizing of plate about the death-bed of a man who had always, after all, shown himself exceedingly affectionate towards the Stonors and devoted to their interests, and who was now my lady's son-in-law. The attempt to make the young wife of sixteen sole executrix, so that she might be completely in her family's hands and without the counsel of two experienced and disinterested merchants, has a somewhat sinister air. The intrigues went on, and three days later the agent writes again. It is pleasant to observe that bad-tempered old Mistress Croke, Dame Elizabeth's mother, was not unmindful of Betson's forbearance during those visits when she had railed upon him with her sharp tongue:

As for the tidings that is here, I trust to God it shall be very good. On Thursday my lady Croke came to Stepney and brought with her Master Brinkley to see Betson, and in faith he was a very sick man; and ere he departed he gave him plasters to his head, to his stomach and to his belly, [so] that he all that night was in a quiet rest. And he came to him again on Friday . . . and he was well amended and so said all the people that were about him. Notwithstanding he will not determine him whether he shall live or die as yet, but he may keep him alive till Tuesday noon, he will undertake him. The cause that I write to you now rather was because I had no certainty. Sir, there hath been many special labours and secret i-made, sithen mistress Jane and I were come, to the contrary disposition that we come for. I cannot write the plain-[nes]s of them as yet, for my mistress Betson attendeth, all things and counsels laid apart, to abide and trust in your good fatherhood and in my lady, and furthermore if he depart the world, ye shall hear tidings of her in as goodly haste as we may purvey for her. And whether he die or live, it is necessary and behoveful that mistress Jane depart not from her into [i.e. until] such time as the certainty be knowen, for in truth divers folks, which ye shall know hereafter and my lady, both thus hath and would exhort her to a contrarier disposition, had not we been here by time. And mistress Jane is worthy of much thank.[29]

However, all the schemings were premature, for Betson happily recovered. On October 10th the "prentice" Henham writes: "My master Betson is right well amended, blessed be Jesus, and he is past all doubts of sickness and he takes the sustenance right well, and as for physicians, there come none unto him, for he hath no need of them." [30] But another death was at hand to break the close association between Thomas Betson and the Stonors, for at the end of the year the kind, extravagant, affectionate Dame Elizabeth died. It is a surprising fact that her death seems to have brought to a close the business partnership between her husband and her son-in-law. Henceforth the only references to Thomas Betson in the Stonor papers are occasional notes of his debts to Stonor: doubtless he had bought Sir William's share in their joint business. On March 10, 1480, he acknowledged obligations of £2,835 9s. od. to Stonor, and in 1482 he still owed £1,200.[31] It is impossible to guess why the relationship, which was an affectionate personal friendship as well as a business tie, should have come to such a sudden end. As the editor of the "Stonor Letters" remarks, "The sincerity and honesty of Betson's character as revealed in his letters, forbids one to suppose that he was to blame."

Such was the more private and domestic side of Thomas Betson's life; but it tells us little (save in occasional references to the Fellowship of the Staple or the price of Cotswold wool) about that great company with which this chapter began; and since he stands here as a type as well as an individual, we must needs turn now to his public and business life, and try to find out from more indirect evidence how a Merchant of the Staple went about his business. The stapler, who would make a good livelihood, must do two things, and give his best attention to both of them: first, he must buy his wool from the English grower, then he must sell it to the foreign buyer. Some of the best wool in England came from the Cotswolds, and when you are a Merchant of the Staple you enjoy bargaining for it, whether you want the proceeds of the great summer clip or of the fells after the autumn sheepkilling. So Thomas Betson rides off to Gloucestershire in the soft spring weather, his good sorrel between his knees, and the scent of the hawthorn blowing round him as he goes. Other wool merchants ride farther afield—into the long dales of Yorkshire to bargain with Cistercian abbots for the wool from their huge flocks, but he and the Celys swear by Cotswold fells (he shipped 2,348 of them to London one July "in the names of Sir William Stonor knight and Thomas Betson, in the 'Jesu' of London, John Lolyngton master under God"). May is the great month for purchases, and Northleach the great meetingplace of staplers and wool dealers. It is no wonder that Northleach Church is so full of woolmen's brasses, for often they knelt there, and often the village hummed with the buyers and sellers, exchanging orders and examining samples. The Celys bought chiefly from two Northleach wool dealers, William Midwinter and John Busshe. The relations between dealers and sellers were often enough close and pleasant: Midwinter even occasionally tried to provide a customer with a bride as well as with a cargo, and marriageable young ladies were not unwilling to be examined over a gallon of wine and much good cheer at the inn.[32] It is true that Midwinter was apt to be restive when his bills remained for too long unpaid, but he may be forgiven for that. Thomas Betson favoured the wool fells of Robert Turbot of Lamberton,[33] and dealt also with one John Tate, with Whyte of Broadway (another famous wool village),[34] and with John Elmes, a Henley merchant well known to the Stonors. Midwinter, Busshe, and Elmes were all wool dealers, or "broggers"—middlemen, that is to say, between the farmers who grew and the staplers who bought wool, but often the staplers dealt directly with individual farmers, buying the

small man's clip as well as the great man's, and warm friend-
ships sprang from the annual visits, looked forward to in
Yorkshire dale and Cotswold valley. It strikes a pleasant note
when Richard Russell, citizen and merchant of York, leaves
in his will, "for distribution among the farmers of Yorkes
Walde, from whom I bought wool 20 l., and in the same way
among the farmers of Lyndeshay 10 l." (1435).[35]

The "Cely Letters" give a mass of information about the
wool buying at Northleach. In the May of the same year in
which Betson's partnership with Stonor would seem to have
ended, old Richard Cely was up there doing business and
reporting it to his son, "Jorge Cely at Caleys."

I greet you well and I have received a letter from you writ
at Calais the 13th day of May (1480), the which letter I have
well understood of your being at the marts and of the sale
of my middle wool, desired by John Destermer and John
Underbay. Wherefore by the grace of God I am a-busied
for to ship this foresaid 29 sarplers, the which I bought of
William Midwinter of Northleach, 26 sarplers, the which is
fair wool, as the wool packer Will Breten saith to me, and
also the 3 sarplers of the rector's is fair wool, much finer wool
nor was the year before, the which I shipped afore Easter
last past. The shipping is begun at London, but I have none
shipped as yet, but I will after these holy days, for the which
I will ye order for the freight and other costs. This same
day your brother Richard Cely is rid to Northleach for to see
and cast a sort of fell for me and another sort of fell for you.[36]

On another occasion he writes: "By your letter you avise me
for to buy wool in Cotswold, for which I shall have of John
Cely his gathering 30 sack, and of Will Midwinter of Northleach 40 sack. And I am avised to buy no more; wool in
Cotswold is at great price, 13s. 4d. a tod, and great riding for
wool in Cotswold as was any year this seven year." [37] What a
picture it calls up of merchants trotting along the roads and
looking as Chaucer often saw them look:

> A Marchant was ther with a forked berd,
> In motteleye and hye on horse he sat,
> Upon his heed a Flaundryssh bever hat,
> His bootes clasped faire and fetisly;
> His resons he spak ful solempnely,
> Sounynge alway thencrees of his wynnyng.

Often at Northleach Betson must have encountered his brethren of the Staple, the staid old merchant Richard Cely among the rest, and son George who rides with "Meg," his hawk, on his wrist, and has a horse called "Bayard" and another called "Py"; and perhaps also John Barton of Holme beside Newark, the proud stapler who set as a "posy" in the stained glass windows of his house this motto:

> I thank God and ever shall
> It is the sheepe hath payed for all;[38]

though indeed it is unlikely that he came as far south as the Cotswolds for his wool. Sometimes also Betson meets upon the road his rivals, stout, self-possessed Flemings and thin sleek Lombards with black eyes and gesticulating hands, who have no business in the Cotswolds at all, but ought to be buying wool in the mart at Calais. But they come, and all good Englishmen are angry at their tricks and angrier still perhaps at their successful trade. "I have not as yet packed my wool in London," writes old Richard Cely on October 29, 1480; "nor have I not bought this year a lock of wool, for the wool of Cotswold is bought by Lombards, wherefore I have the less haste for to pack my wool at London";[39] and his son writes to him on November 16th from Calais: "There is but little Cotswold wool at Calais and I understand Lombards has bought it up in England." [40] It is true that the Celys, other English merchants too, are not unwilling to conclude private bargains from time to time with foreign buyers in England. Two years later their agent, William Cely, writes to advise them that two Flemish merchants are now trying to buy in England contrary to the ordinance, and that those in authority at Calais have got wind of it, and therefore his

masters must take care and make Wyllykyn and Peter Bale
pay at Calais, "but as for your dealings knoweth no man,
without they search Peter Bales' books." [41] The upright Betson no doubt eschewed such tricks and resented particularly
the clever usurious Lombards, so full of financial dodges to
trick the English merchant, for did they not buy the wool in
England on credit, riding about as they list in the Cotswolds?

> In Cotteswolde also they ryde aboute
> And al Englonde, and bien wythouten doute,
> What them liste, wythe fredome and fraunchise
> More then we Englisshe may getyn in any wyse.

And then did they not carry the wool to Flanders and sell
it for ready money at a loss of five per cent, thereafter lending
out this money at heavy usury, mostly to the English merchants themselves, so that by the time pay day came in England, they had realized a heavy profit?

> And thus they wold, if we will beleve
> Wypen our nose with our owne sleve,
> Thow this proverbe be homly and undew,
> Yet be liklynesse it is forsoth fulle trew. [42]

The next serious piece of business Thomas Betson must
take in hand is the packing and shipping of his wool to Calais.
Here he found himself enmeshed in the regulations of the
company and the Crown, ever on the look-out for fraud in
the packing or description of the staple product. The wool
had to be packed in the county from which it came, and there
were strict regulations against mixing hair and earth or rub-
bish with it. The collectors appointed by the company for the
different wool-growing districts, and sworn in before the ex-
chequer, rode round and sealed each package, so that it could
not be opened without breaking the seal. Then the great bales
were carried on the backs of pack-horses "by the ancient track-
ways over the Wiltshire and Hampshire Downs, which had
been used before the Roman conquest, and thence through
Surrey and Kent to the Medway ports by the Pilgrims' Way."
At the different ports the collectors of customs were ready to

enter on their rolls the names of the merchants shipping wool, together with the quantity and description of wool shipped by each.[43] Some of the wool came to London itself, where many of the staplers had offices in Mark Lane (which is a corruption of Mart Lane), and was weighed for the assessment of the customs and subsidy at the Leadenhall.[44] In this business Thomas Betson was helped by Stonor's three assistants or "prentices," as they call themselves, Thomas Henham, Goddard Oxbridge, and Thomas Howlake, for the last of whom he had a warm corner in his heart, because the young man was gentle to little Katherine Riche. These men were sometimes at the Stonors' London warehouse and sometimes at their house in Calais, and they saved Betson a good deal of trouble, being experienced enough to oversee both the packing of wool in London and its sale in Calais.

To Calais the wool thus packed, and weighed and marked and assessed by the customs officer, was carried in the ships of Calais itself, or of the little ports on the east or southeastern coast of England, many of which are mere villages to-day. For ships put out not only from Hull and Colchester, but from Brightlingsea, Rotherhithe, Walberswick in Suffolk, Rainham in Essex, Bradwell, Maidstone, Milton, Newhithe, and Milhall. In August, 1478, the Celys were paying the masters of twenty-one different ships for the freight of their sarplers of wool after the summer clip.[45] All through the summer the shipping went on, and right up to Christmas; but during the winter months the merchants were mostly sending over fells or sheepskins, after the great slaughter of sheep and cattle which took place at Martinmas, when housewives salted down their meat for the winter and farmers made delivery of the fells and hides, for which the staplers had long ago bargained. Very often merchants' letters and customs accounts give us the names of these doughty little ships and their cargoes. In the October of 1481, for instance, the Celys were shipping a consignment of fells:

Right worshipful sir, after due recommendation I lowly recommend unto you, letting you understand that my master hath shipped his fells at the port of London now at this shipping in October . . . , which fells ye must receive and pay the freight first by the grace of God, in the "Mary" of London, William Sordyvale master, 7 packs, sum 2800, lying be aft the mast, one pack lieth up rest and some of that pack is summer fells marked with an O, and then lieth 3 packs fells of William Daltons and under them lieth the other 6 packs of my masters. Item in the "Christopher" of Rainham, Harry Wylkyns master, 7 packs and a half Cots-[wold] fell, sum 3000 pelt, lying be aft the mast, and under them lieth a 200 fells of Welther Fyldes, William Lyndys man of Northampton, and the partition is made with small cords. Item, in the "Thomas" of Maidstone, Harry Lawson master, 6 pokes, sum 2400 pelt, whereof lieth 5 packs next before the mast under hatches, no man above them, and one pack lieth in the stern sheet; of the six packs fells be some summer fells marked with an O likewise. Item, in the "Mary Grace" of London, John Lokyngton master 6 packs, sum 2400 pelt, lying be aft under the fells of Thomas Graunger, the partition between them is made with red; sum of the fells my master hath shipped at this time 26 packs and a half whereof be winter fells of the country 561 fells and they be marked with an C, and of summer fells there should be 600 and more, but part of them be left behind, for we have two packs we could have no appointment for them, and all the summer fells be marked with an O. Item, sir, ye shall receive of the "Mary" of Rainham, John Danyell master, your *male* [trunk] with your gear and a Essex cheese marked with my master's mark.

And so on, with details of the number of fells shipped in like manner by the "Michael" of Hull and the "Thomas" of Newhithe, where they lay "next the mast aftward under the fells of Thomas Betson's," over 11,000 fells in all.[46]

How invigorating is such a list of ships. Cargoes are the most romantic of topics, whether they be apes and ivory and peacocks, or "cheap tin trays"; and since the day that Jason sailed to Colchis fleeces have ever been among the most romantic of cargoes. How they smack of the salt too, those old master mariners, Henry Wilkins, master of the "Christopher" of Rainham, John Lollington master of the "Jesu" of London, Robert Ewen, master of the "Thomas" of Newhithe, and all the rest of them, waving their hands to their wives and sweethearts as they sail out of the sparkling little bays, with the good woolsacks abaft or under hatches—shipmen, all of them, after Chaucer's heart:

> But of his craft, to rekene wel his tydes
> His stremes and his daungers hym besides,
> His herberwe and his moone, his lodemenage,
> Ther was noon swich from Hulle to Cartage.
> Hardy he was, and wys to undertake:
> With many a tempest hadde his berd been shake;
> He knew wel alle the havenes, as they were,
> From Gootland to the Cape of Fynystere,
> And every cryke in Britaigne and in Spayne.
> His barge y-cleped was the Maudelayne.

Their ships were doubtless like the "Margaret Cely," which the two Cely brothers bought and called after their mother, for the not excessive sum of £28, exclusive of rigging and fittings. She carried a master, boatswain, cook, and sixteen jolly sailormen, and she kept a good look out for pirates and was armed with cannon and bows, bills, five dozen darts, and twelve pounds of gunpowder! She was victualled with salt fish, bread, wheat, and beer, and she plied with the Celys' trade to Zealand, Flanders, and Bordeaux.[47] She must have been about two hundred tons, but some of the other little ships were much smaller, for, as the learned editor of the "Cely Papers" tells us, "The ships of the little Medway ports could scarcely have been of thirty tons to navigate the river safely; the 'Thomas' of Maidstone can have been only a barge, if she had to pass Aylesford Bridge."[48] But they navigated the channel and dodged the pirates blithely enough, though often Thomas Betson at Calais was nervous about the safe arrival of the wool fleet. Like Chaucer's merchant,

> He wolde the see were kept for any thing
> Betwixe Middelburgh and Orewelle.

Side by side with George or Richard Cely he must often have strained his eyes from the quay, with the salt wind blowing out the feather in his cap, and breathed a thanksgiving to God when the ships hove in sight. "And, Sir," he writes once to Stonor from London, "thanked be the good Lord, I understand for certain that our wool shipped be comen in . . . to Calais. I would have kept the tidings till I had comen myself, because it is good, but I durst not be so bold, for your mastership now against this good time may be glad and joyful of these tidings, for in truth I am glad and heartily thank God of it." [49] The "prentice" Thomas Henham writes likewise three weeks later: "I departed from Sandwich the 11th day of April and so came unto Calais upon Sher Thursday* last with the wool ships, and so blessed be Jesu I have received your wools in safety. Furthermore, Sir, if it please your mastership for to understand this, I have received your wools as fair and as whole as any man's in the fleet. Moreover, Sir, if it please your mastership for to understand how your wool was housed ever deal by Easter even. Furthermore, Sir, if it please your mastership for to understand that the shipman be content and paid of their freight." [50] The Celys write in the same strain too: "This day the 16th of August the wool fleet came to Calais both of London and Ipswich in safety, thanked be God, and this same day was part landed and it riseth fair yet, thanked be God." [51] Their letters tell us too what danger it was that they feared. "I pray Jesu send you safe hither and soon," writes Richard to his "right well beloved brother George," on June 6, 1482. "Robert Eryke was chased with Scots between Calais and Dover. They scaped narrow." [52] There are many such chases recorded, and we hear too of wool burnt under hatches or cast overboard in a storm.[53]

Thomas Betson and the Celys travelled very often across the Channel in these ships, which carried passengers and letters, and they were almost as much at home in Calais as in London. When in Calais English merchants were not allowed to live anywhere they liked, all over the town. The Company

* I.e. Shrove Thursday.

of the Staple had a list of regular licensed "hosts," in whose
houses they might stay. Usually a number of merchants lived
with each host, the most potent, grave, and reverend seniors
dining at a high table, and smaller fry at side tables in the
hall. Sometimes they quarrelled over terms, as when William
Cely writes home one day to Richard and George in London:

Item. Sir, please it you to understand that here is a
variance betwixt our host Thomas Graunger and the fellowship, of our lodging, for Thomas Graunger promised us at
his coming in to our lodging that we should pay no more for
our board but 3s. 4d. a week at the high table, and 2s. 6d.
at the side table, and now he saith he will have no less than
4s. a week at the high table and 40d. at the side table, wherefore the fellowship here will depart into other lodgings, some
to one place and some to another. William Dalton will be
at Robert Torneys and Ralph Temyngton and master Brown's
man of Stamford shall be at Thomas Clarke's and so all the
fellowship departs save I, wherefore I let your masterships
have knowledge, that ye may do as it shall like you best.[54]

But Thomas Betson never fell out with his hosts, whose only
complaint of him must have been that he sat long over his
love letters and came down late to dinner.

There was business enough for him to do at Calais. First
of all, when the wool was landed, it had to be inspected by
the Royal officers, to see that it had been properly labelled,
and their skilled packers examined, repacked, and resealed
the bales. This was an anxious moment for merchants who
were conscious of inferior wool among their bulging sarplers.
The honest Betson, we may be certain, never cheated, but the
Celys knew more than a little about the tricks of the trade,
and one year, when the Lieutenant of Calais took out sarpler
No. 24, which their agent, William Cely, knew to be poor
wool, in order to make a test, he privily substituted No. 8,
which was "fair wool" and changed the labels, so that he was
soon able to write home, "Your wool is awarded by the sarpler
that I cast out last." [55] No wonder Gower said that Trick was
regent of the Staple,

Siq'en le laines maintenir
Je voi plusours descontenir
Du loyalté la viele usance.[56]

Then there was the custom and subsidy to be paid to the
Mayor and Fellowship of the Staple, who collected it for the
King. And then came the main business of every merchant
the selling of the wool. Thomas Betson preferred, of course
to sell it as quickly as possible, as the ships came in, but some
times the market was slow and wool remained for some
months on his hands. Such wool from the summer sheep shear
ing, shipped in or before the month of February following
and remaining unsold by April 6th, was classed as old wool
and the Fellowship of the Staple ordained that foreign buyer
must take one sarpler of old wool with every three of new
and although the Flemings grumbled and wanted to take one
of old to five of new, they had to put up with the regulation.[57]
A great deal of Betson's business would be done at the mart o
Calais itself, where he met with the dignified Flemish mer
chants, scions of old families with estates of their own, and the
more plebeian merchants of Delft and Leyden, and the woo
dealers from sunny Florence and Genoa and Venice. Among
the best customers both of the Stonors and the Celys (fo
they are mentioned in the letters of both) were Peter and
Daniel van de Rade of Bruges. Thomas Howlake on one oc
casion reports a sale of four sarplers of fine Cotswold woo
to them at 19 marks the sack, with a rebate of 4½ cloves on
the sack of 52, and adds: "Sir, an it please you, as for the
foresaid merchants that have bought your wool, [they] be a
good as any that came out of Flanders and for that I have
showed them the more favour and given them the more res
pite of that." [58]

The staplers, however, did not do business at Calais alone
but rode also to the great fairs at Antwerp, Bruges, and the
country round. "Thomas Betson," writes Henham to hi
master, "came unto Calais the last day of April and so h
departed in good health unto Bruges mart the first day o
May." [59]

> But so bifel this marchant on a day
> Shoop hym to make redy his array
> Toward the toun of Brugges for to fare,
> To byen there a porcioun of ware—60

only it was to "sellen" a portion that Betson went. He himself writes Sir William: "Liketh it you to wit that on Trinity
even I came to Calais and, thanked be the good Lord, I had
a full fair passage, and, Sir, with God's might I intend on
Friday next to depart to the mart-wards. I beseech the good
Lord be my speed and help me in all my works. And, Sir, I
trust to God's mercy, if the world be merry here, to do somewhat that shall be both to your profit and mine. As yet there
cometh but few merchants here; hereafter with God's grace
there will come more. I shall lose no time when the season
shall come, I promise you. . . . And, Sir, when I come from
the mart I shall send you word of all matters by the mercy of
our Lord." 61 At the fairs Betson would meet with a great
crowd of merchants from all over Europe, though often
enough political disturbances made the roads dangerous and
merchants ran some risk of being robbed. The English traders
were commonly reputed to be the best sellers and customers
at the fairs of Flanders and Brabant, though the Flemings
sometimes complained of them, and said that the staplers
made regulations forbidding their merchants to buy except
on the last day, when the Flemish sellers, anxious to pack
and be off, let their goods go at insuffient prices.62 The author of the *Libelle of Englysshe Polycye* boasts proudly of the
custom brought by the English to these marts:

> But they of Holonde at Calyse byene oure felles,
> And oure wolles, that Englyshe men hem selles . . .
> And wee to martis of Braban charged bene
> Wyth Englysshe clothe, fulle gode and feyre to seyne,
> Wee bene ageyne charged wyth mercerye
> Haburdasshere ware and wyth grocerye,
> To whyche martis, that Englisshe men call feyres
> Iche nacion ofte makethe here repayeres,
> Englysshe and Frensh, Lumbards, Januayes [Genoese],

Cathalones, theder take here wayes,
Scottes, Spaynardes, Iresshmen there abydes,
Wythe grete plente bringing of salt hydes,
And I here saye that we in Braban lye,
Flaunders and Seland, we bye more marchaundy
In common use, then done all other nacions;
This have I herde of marchaundes relacions,
And yff the Englysshe be not in the martis,
They bene febelle and as nought bene here partes;
For they bye more and fro purse put owte
More marchaundy than alle other rowte.[63]

Fairs were held at different times in different places, but
there were during the year four great fair seasons, corresponding to the four seasons in the year.[64] There was the Cold
mart in the winter, to which Thomas Betson rode muffled in
fur, with his horse's hoofs ringing on the frosty roads; there
was the Pask (*Pasques*, Easter) mart in the spring, when he
whistled blithely and stuck a violet in his cap; there was the
Synxon (St. John) mart in the summer, round about St. John
the Baptist's Day, when he was hot and mopped his brow,
and bought a roll of tawny satin or Lucca silk for Katherine
from a Genoese in a booth at Antwerp; and there was the
Balms, or Bammys mart in the autumn, round about the day
of St. Rémy, whom the Flemings call St. Bamis (October
28), when he would buy her a fur of budge or mink, or a
mantle of fine black shanks from the Hansards at their mart
in Bruges. It was at these marts that the Merchants of the
Staple, jaunting about from place to place to meet buyers
for their wool, did a hundred little commissions for their
friends; for folk at home were apt to think that staplers existed
to do their errands for them abroad and to send them presents.
One wanted a pair of Louvain gloves, the other a sugar loaf,
the other a pipe of Gascon wine ("You can get it cheaper
over there, my dear"), the other a yard or two of Holland
cloth; while ginger and saffron were always welcome, and
could be bought from the Venetians, whom the Celys spell
"Whenysyans." Then, of course, there were purchases to be

made in the way of business, such as Calais pack-thread and canvas from Arras or Brittany or Normandy to pack the bales of wool.[65] As to the Celys, Thomas Betson was wont to say that their talk was of nothing but sport and buying hawks, save on one gloomy occasion, when George Cely rode for ten miles in silence and then confided to him that over in England his grey bitch had whelped and had fourteen pups, and then died and the pups with her.[66]

Between the counting-house in Calais and the fairs and marts of the country Thomas Betson would dispose of his wool and fells. But his labour did not end here, for he would now have to embark upon the complicated business of collecting money from his customers, the Flemish merchants, and with it paying his creditors in England, the Cotswold wool dealers. It was customary for the staplers to pay for their wool by bills due, as a rule, at six months, and Thomas Betson would be hard put to meet them if the foreign buyers delayed to pay him. Moreover, his difficulties were inconceivably complicated by the exchanges. We think we know something about the difficulty of divers and fluctuating exchanges to-day, but we can hardly imagine the elaborate calculations and the constant disputes which racked the brain of a Merchant of the Staple in the fifteenth century. Not only did the rates between England and the Continent constantly vary, but, as the editor of the "Cely Papers" points out, "the number of potentates of all kinds who claimed the privilege of issuing their own coinage and the frequently suspicious character of what they uttered as gold and silver, made the matter of adjustment of values difficult for the Celys, who were evidently obliged to take what they could get." [67] Only imagine the difficulties of poor Thomas Betson, when into his counting-house there wandered in turn the Andrew guilder of Scotland, the Arnoldus gulden of Gueldres (very much debased), the Carolus groat of Charles of Burgundy, new crowns and old crowns of France, the David and the Falewe of the Bishopric of Utrecht, the Hettinus groat of the Counts of Westphalia, the Lewe or French Louis d'or, the Limburg groat, the Milan groat, the Nimueguen groat, the Phelippus or Philippe d'or of Brabant, the Plaques of Utrecht, the Postlates of various bishops, the English Ryall (worth ten shillings), the Scots Rider or the Rider of Burgundy (so called because they bore the figure of a man on horseback), the Florin Rhenau of the Bishopric of Cologne and the Setillers.[68] He had to know the value in English money of them all, as it was fixed for the time being by the Fellowship, and most of them were debased past all reason. Indeed, English money enjoyed an enviable good fame in this respect until Henry VIII began debasing the coinage for his own nefarious ends. The letters of the Celys are full of worried references to the exchange, and much we should pity Thomas Betson. But doubtless he was like Chaucer's bearded merchant: "Wel koude he in exchaunge sheeldes [French crowns] selle."

To effect their payments between England and the Netherlands the staplers used to make use of the excellent banking facilities and instruments of credit (bills of exchange and so forth), which were placed at their disposal by Italian and Spanish merchants and by the English mercers, all of whom combined trading with financial operations. Thus we find William Cely writing to his masters:

Please your masterships to understand that I have received of John Delowppys upon payment of the bill, the which is sent me by Adlington but £300 fleming, whereof I have paid to Gynott Strabant £84 6s. 6d. fleming. Item, I have made you over by exchange with Benynge Decasonn, Lombard, 180 nobles sterling, payable at usuance. I delivered it at 11s. 2½d. fleming the noble, it amounteth £100 17s. 6d. fleming. Item, I have made you over by exchange in like wise with Jacob van de Base 89 nobles and 6s. sterling, payable at London at usuance in like wise; I delivered it at 11s. 2d. fleming for every noble sterling; it amounteth fl.—£50 fleming and the rest of your £300 remains still by me, for I can make you over no more at this season, for here is no more that will take any money as yet. And money goeth now upon the bourse at 11s. 3½d. the noble and none other money but Nimueguen groats, crowns, Andrew guilders and Rhenish guilders, and the exchange goeth ever the longer worse and worse. Item, sir, I send you enclosed in this said letter, the two first letters of the payment of the exchange above written. Benynge Decasonn's letter is directed to Gabriel Defuye and Peter Sanly, Genoese, and Jacob van de Base's is directed to Anthony Carsy and Marcy Strossy, Spaniards; in Lombard Street ye shall hear of them.[69]

A week later he writes:

I understand your masterships hath taken up by exchange of John Raynold, mercer, £60 sterling, payable the 25th day of the month and of Deago Decastron [Diego da Castro, a Spaniard] other £60 sterling, payable the 26th day of the same month, the which shall be both content at the day; and as for master Lewis More, Lombard, [he] is paid and I have the bill; his attorney is a wrangling fellow—he would none other money but Nimueguen groats.[70]

Many a letter such as this must Thomas Betson have written at his lodgings, sitting so late over his work that he must needs write to his friends when he ought to be sleeping and date his letters: "At London, on our Lady day in the night, when I deem ye were in your bed, for mine eyne smarted, so God help me."[71] And when he came to make up his annual accounts he had the hardest work of all to do. Here is a portrait of him at his labours:

> The thridde day this marchant up ariseth,
> And on his nedes sadly hym avyseth,
> And up into his countour-hous gooth he,
> To rekene with hymself, as wel may be,
> Of thilke yeer, how that it with hym stood,
> And how that he despended hadde his good,
> And if that he encressed were or noon.
> His bookes and his bagges, many oon,
> He leith biforn hym on his countyng-bord.
> Ful riche was his tresor and his hord,
> For which ful faste his countour dore he shette;
> And eek he nolde that no man sholde hym lette

Of his accountes, for the meene tyme;
And thus he sit til it was passed pryme.[72]

Thus was passed the life of a Merchant of the Staple:
in riding to the Cotswold farms for wool; in business at the
counting-houses in Mark's Lane; in sailing from London to
Calais and from Calais to London again; in dealing with merchant strangers at the mart in Calais, or riding to the marts
of Flanders in fair time. The great company sheltered him,
arranged his lodging, kept a sharp eye on the quality of his
wool, made rules for his buying and selling, and saw that he
had justice in its court. It was in this setting of hard and
withal of interesting work that Thomas Betson's love story
flowered into a happy marriage. He was not destined to live
long after his recovery from the serious illness of 1479; perhaps it left him permanently delicate, for he died some six
years later, in 1486. During her seven years of married life
(beginning, be it remembered, at the age of fifteen), the
diligent Katherine had borne him five children, two sons,
Thomas and John, and three daughters, Elizabeth, Agnes, and
Alice. Fortunately Thomas died very comfortably off, as his
will (still preserved in Somerset House) informs us. He had
become a member of the Fishmongers' Company as well as a
Merchant of the Staple, for by his time the great city companies were no longer confined to persons actually engaged in
the trade which each represented. In his will[73] Thomas Betson leaves money for the repair of the rood loft in his parish
church of All Hallows, Barking, where he was buried, and
"thirty pounds to the garnishing of the Staple Chapel in Our
Lady Church at Calais, to buy some jewel," and twenty
pounds to the "Stockfishmongers" to buy plate. He makes the
latter company the guardian of his children, leaves his two
houses to his wife, and a legacy of 40s. to Thomas Henham,
his colleague in Stonor's service, and characteristically gives
directions "for the costs of my burying to be done not outrageously, but soberly and discreetly and in a mean [mod-
erate, medium] manner, that it may be unto the worship and
laud of Almighty God." Katherine, a widow with five children

at the age of twenty-two, married as her second husband
William Welbech, haberdasher (the Haberdashers were a
wealthy company), by whom she had another son. But her
heart stayed with the husband who wrote her her first playful
love-letter when she was a child, and on her death in 1510 she
directed that she should be laid by the side of Thomas Betson
at All Hallows, Barking, where three staplers still lie beneath
their brasses, although no trace of him remains.[74] There let
them lie, long forgotten, and yet worthier of memory than
many of the armoured knights who sleep under carved sep-
ulchres in our beautiful medieval churches.

> The garlands wither on your brow;
>   Then boast no more your mighty deeds!
> Upon Death's purple altar now
>   See where the victor-victim bleeds.
>   Your heads must come
>   To the cold tomb:
> Only the actions of the just
> Smell sweet and blossom in their dust.

CHAPTER VI

THOMAS PAYCOCKE OF COGGESHALL

An Essex Clothier in the Days of Henry VII

> This was a gallant cloathier sure
> Whose fame for ever shall endure.
> —THOMAS DELONEY

THE great and noble trade of cloth-making has left many traces upon the life of England, architectural, literary, and social. It has filled our countryside with magnificent Perpendicular churches and gracious oak-beamed houses. It has filled our popular literature with old wives' tales of the worthies of England, in which the clothiers Thomas of Reading and Jack of Newbury rub elbows with Friar Bacon and Robin Hood. It has filled our shires with gentlemen; for, as Defoe observed, in the early eighteenth century "many of the great families who now pass for gentry in the western counties have been originally raised from and built up by this truly noble manufacture." It has filled our census lists with surnames—Weaver, Webber, Webb, Sherman, Fuller, Walker, Dyer—and given to every unmarried woman the designation of a spinster. And from the time when the cloth trade ousted that of wool as the chief export trade of England down to the time when it was in its turn ousted by iron and cotton, it was the foundation of England's commercial greatness. "Among all Crafts," says old Deloney, "this was the only chief, for that it was the greatest merchandize, by the which our Country became famous thorowout all Nations." [1]

Already by the end of the fourteenth century the English clothiers were beginning to rival those of the Netherlands in the making of fine cloth, as witness Chaucer's Wife of Bath:

> Of clooth-making she hadde swiche an haunt
> She passed hem of Ypres and of Gaunt,

and by the end of the sixteenth century all real rivalry was at an end, for the English manufacture was so clearly victorious. With the development of the manufacture a change too took place in its organization. It had never been an easy industry to organize on a gild basis, because the making of a piece of cloth entailed so many distinct processes. The preliminary processes of spinning and carding were always by-industries, performed by women and children in their cottages; but the weavers, who bought the spun yarn, had their gild; and so had the fullers, who fulled it; and the shearmen, who finished it; and the dyers, who dyed it. All could not sell the finished piece of cloth, and in the group of inter-dependent crafts, each with its gild, we sometimes find the weavers employing the fullers and sometimes the fullers the weavers. Moreover, since weaving is a much quicker process than spinning, the weaver often wasted much time and found it hard to collect enough yarn to keep his loom busy; and, as the market for cloth grew wider and was no longer confined to the town of the weaver, the need was felt for some middleman to specialize in the selling of the finished cloth. So by degrees there grew up a class of men who bought wool in large quantities and sold it to the weavers, and then by a natural transition began, not to sell the wool outright, but to deliver it to the weavers to weave, to the fullers to full, and to the shearmen to finish at a wage, receiving it back again when the work was done. These men grew rich; they amassed capital; they could set many folk at work. Soon they began to set to work all the different workers who combined to make a piece of cloth; their servants carried wool to the cottages for the women to card and spin; carried the spun yarn in turn to dyers, weavers, fullers, shearers; and carried the finished piece of cloth back to the industrial middleman—the clothier, as he was called—who in his turn disposed of it to the mercantile middleman, who was called a draper. The clothiers grew rapidly in wealth and importance, and in certain parts of the country became the backbone of the middle class. They pursued their activities in country villages, rather than in the old corporate towns, for they wished to avoid the restrictions of the gilds, and gradually the cloth industry migrated almost entirely to the country. In the west of England and in East Anglia (though not in Yorkshire) it was carried out by clothiers on this "putting out" system, right up to the moment when the Industrial Revolution swept it out of the cottages into the factories and out of the south into the north. Then the thriving villages emptied themselves, so that to-day we must needs re-create again from scattered traces and old buildings, and still older names, the once familiar figures of the East Anglian clothier and his swarm of busy workmen.

Such a familiar figure was once old Thomas Paycocke, clothier, of Coggeshall in Essex, who died full of years and honour in 1518. His family originally came from Clare, in Suffolk, but about the middle of the fifteenth century a branch settled at Coggeshall, a village not far distant. His grandfather and father would seem to have been grazing butchers, but he and his brother and their descendants after them followed "the truly noble manufacture" of cloth-making, and set an indelible mark upon the village where they dwelt. Coggeshall lies in the great cloth-making district of Essex, of which Fuller wrote: "This county is charactered like Bethsheba, 'She layeth her hand to the spindle and her hands hold the distaffe.' . . . It will not be amiss to pray that the plough may go along and the wheel around, that so (being fed by the one and clothed by the other) there may be, by God's blessing, no danger of starving in our nation." [2] All over Essex there lay villages famous for cloth-making, Coggeshall and Braintree, Bocking and Halstead, Shalford and Dedham, and above all Colchester, the great centre and mart of the trade. The villages throve on the industry and there was hardly a cottage which did not hum with the spinning wheel, and hardly a street where you might not have counted weavers' workshops, kitchens where the rough loom stood by the wall to occupy the goodman's working hours. Hardly a week but the clatter of the pack-horse would be heard in the straggling streets, bringing in new stores of wool to be worked and taking away the pieces of cloth to the clothiers of Colchester and the surrounding villages. Throughout the fifteenth century Coggeshall was an important centre, second only to the great towns of Norwich, Colchester, and Sudbury, and to this day its two inns are called the "Woolpack" and the "Fleece." We must, as I said, build up the portrait of Thomas Paycocke and his compeers from scattered traces; but happily such traces are common enough in many and many an English village, and in Coggeshall itself they lie ready to our hand. Out of three things he can be brought to life again—to wit, his house in the village street, his family brasses in the aisle of the village church, and his will, which is preserved at Somerset House. A house, a brass, a will—they seem little enough, but they hold all his history. It is the greatest error to suppose that history must needs be something written down; for it may just as well be something built up, and churches, houses, bridges, or amphitheatres can tell their story as plainly as print for those who have eyes to read. The Roman villa, excavated after lying lost for centuries beneath the heel of the unwitting ploughboy—that villa with its spacious ground-plan, its floors rich with mosaic patterns, its elaborate heating apparatus, and its shattered vases, brings home more clearly than any textbook the real meaning of the Roman Empire, whose citizens lived like this in a foggy island at the uttermost edge of its world. The Norman castle, with moat and drawbridge, gatehouse and bailey and keep, arrow slits instead of windows, is more eloquent than a hundred chronicles of the perils of life in the twelfth century; not thus dwelt the private gentleman in the days of Rome. The country manor-house of the fourteenth century, with courtyard and chapel and hall and dovecote, speaks of an age of peace once more, when life on a thousand little manors revolved round the lord, and the great mass of Englishmen went unscathed by the Hundred Years' War which seamed the fair face of France. Then begin the merchants' elaborate Perpendicular houses in the towns and villages of the fifteenth century, standing on the road, with gardens behind them, and carved beams, great fire-places, and a general air of comfort; they mark the advent of a new class in English history—the middle class, thrust between lord and peasant and coming to its own.

How the spacious days of great Elizabeth are mirrored in the beautiful Elizabethan houses, with their wide wings and large rooms, their chimneys, their glass windows, looking outwards on to open parks and spreading trees, instead of inwards on to the closed courtyard. Or go into a house built or redecorated in the eighteenth century, where you will see Chippendale chairs and lacquer tables and Chinese wall-papers covered with pagodas and mandarins; and surely there will come to your mind the age of the nabobs, the age which John Company had familiarized with the products of the Far East, the age in which tea ousted coffee as the drink for a gentleman of fashion, in which Horace Walpole collected porcelain, Oliver Goldsmith idealized China in "The Citizen of the World," and Dr. Johnson was called the Great Cham of Literature. Look here upon this picture and on this: look at that row of jerry-built houses, a hundred in a row and all exactly alike, or that new-art villa, all roof and hardly any window, with false bottle glass in its panes; here is the twentieth century for you. Indeed all the social and very much of the political history of England may be reconstructed from her architecture alone; and so I make no apology for calling Thomas Paycocke's house first-rate historical evidence.

Of much the same type, though less interesting, is the evidence of monumental brasses, which are to be found in most parts of England and which abound in East Anglia, the Home Counties, and the Thames Valley.[3] Their variety is magnificent: brasses of ecclesiastics in vestments, of doctors of law and divinity and masters of arts in academic dress and of a few abbots and abbesses; brasses of knights in armour; brasses of ladies, with their little dogs at their feet and dresses which show the changes in fashion from century to century and make clear all the mysteries of kirtles and cottehardies, wimples and partlets and farthingales and the head-dresses appropriate to each successive mode. The brasses also, like the houses, bear witness to the prosperity of the middle class, for in the fourteenth century when merchants began to build themselves fine houses they began also to bury themselves under splendid brasses. Finest of all, perhaps, are the brasses of the wool staplers, with feet resting on woolpack or sheep; but there are many other merchants too. Mayors and aldermen abound; they set their merchants' marks upon their tombs as proudly as gentlemen set their coats of arms, and indeed they had as great cause for pride. You may see them at their proudest in the famous brass at Lynn, where Robert Braunch lies between his two wives, and at his feet is incised a scene representing the feast at which he entertained Edward III royally and feasted him on peacocks. There is a tailor with his shears, as glorious as the Crusader's sword, at Northleach, and a wine merchant with his feet upon a wine cask at Cirencester. There are smaller folk too, less dowered with wealth but proud enough of the implements of their craft; two or three public notaries with penhorn and pencase complete, a huntsman with his horn, and in Newland Church one of the free miners of the Forest of Dean, cap and leather breeches tied below the knee, wooden mine-hod over shoulder, a small mattock in his right hand, and a candlestick between his teeth. This kind of historical evidence will help us with Thomas Paycocke. His family brasses were set in the north aisle of the parish church of St. Peter Ad Vincula. Several of them have disappeared in the course of the last century and a half, and unluckily no brass of Thomas himself survives; but in the aisle there still lie two—the brass of his brother John, who died in 1533, and John's wife, and that of his nephew, another Thomas, who died in 1580; the merchant's mark may still be seen thereon.

Lastly, there is the evidence of the Paycocke wills, of which three are preserved at Somerset House—the will of John Paycocke (d. 1505), Thomas's father and the builder of the house; the will of Thomas Paycocke himself (d. 1518); and the will of his nephew Thomas, the same whose brass lies in the aisle and who left a long and splendidly detailed testament, full of information upon local history and the organization of the cloth industry. For social historians have as yet hardly, perhaps, made as much use as they might of the evidence of wills. The enormous amount of miscellaneous information to be derived therefrom about the life of our forefathers can hardly be believed, save by those who have turned the pages of such a collection as the great *Testamenta Eboracen ia*.[4] In wills you may see how many daughters a man could dower and how many he put into a nunnery, and what education he provided for his sons. You may note which were the most popular religious houses, and which men had books and what the books were, how much of their money they thought fit to leave for charitable purposes, and what they thought of the business capacity of their wives. You may read long and dazzling lists of family plate, all the favourite cups and dishes having pet names of their own, and of rings and brooches and belts and rosaries. There are detailed descriptions of dresses and furs, sometimes splendid, sometimes ordinary, for people handed on their rich clothes as carefully as their jewels. There are even more wonderful descriptions of beds, with all their bedclothes and hangings, for a bed was a very valuable article of furniture and must often, judging from the wills, have been a brilliant and beautiful object indeed; Shakespeare has earned a great deal of unmerited obloquy for leaving Ann Hathaway his second-best bed, though it is not to be denied that he might have left her his first-best. Even more beautiful than dressings and bed or chamber hangings are the brocaded and embroidered vestments mentioned in wills, and the elaborate arrangements for funeral ceremonies are extremely interesting. The wills are of all kinds; there are even villeins' wills, though in theory the villein's possessions were his lord's, and there are wills of kings and queens, lords and ladies, bishops and parsons and lawyers and shopkeepers. Here also is more evidence for the social prosperity of the middle class, details of their trade, the contents of their shops, the inventories of their houses, their estates (sometimes) in the country, their house rents (almost always) in the town, their dressers garnished with plate and their wives' ornaments, their apprentices and their gilds, their philanthropy, their intermarriage with the gentry, their religious opinions. Such a living picture do men's wills give us of their daily lives.

These, then, are the three sources from which the life and

times of Thomas Paycocke may be drawn. All three—houses, brasses, and wills—contain much evidence for the increasingly rapid growth during the last two centuries of the Middle Ages of a large and prosperous middle class, whose wealth was based not upon landed property but upon industry and trade. It is a class of whom we have already met typical examples in Thomas Betson and the anonymous Ménagier de Paris, and we must now see what his house, his will, and his family brasses tell us about the clothier Thomas Paycocke. First and foremost, they tell us a great deal about the noble industry which supported him. Paycocke's house is full of relics of the cloth industry. The merchant mark of the Paycockes, an ermine tail, looking like a two-stemmed clover leaf, is to be found on the carved beams of the chimney, on the breast-summers of the fire-places, and set in the midst of the strip of carving along the front of the house. Thomas marked his bales of cloth thus, and what other armorial bearings did he need? The whole house is essentially middle class—the house of a man who was *nouveau riche* in an age when to be *nouveau riche* was not yet to be vulgar. His prosperity has blossomed out into exquisitely ornate decoration. A band of carving runs along the front of the house, and from the curved stem of it branch out a hundred charming devices—leaves, tendrils, strange flowers, human heads, Tudor roses, a crowned king and queen lying hand in hand, a baby diving with a kick of fat legs into the bowl of an arum lily, and in the midst the merchant's mark upon a shield and the initials of the master of the house. In the hall is a beautiful ceiling of carved oakwood, exceedingly elaborate and bearing at intervals the merchant's mark again. Upstairs in the big bed-chamber is a ceiling of beams worked in bold roll mouldings; and there is an exquisite little parlour, lined with linen fold panels, with a breastsummer carved with strange animals. This elaboration is characteristic. It is all of a piece with Coggeshall Church, and with all those other spacious East Anglian churches, Lavenham, Long Melford, Thaxted, Saffron Walden, Lynn, Snettisham, lofty and spacious, which the clothiers built out of their newly won wealth. The very architecture is characteristic, *nouveau riche* again, like those who paid for it, the elaborate ornament and sumptuous detail of the Perpendicular taking the place of the simple majesty of the Early English style. It is just the sort of architecture that a merchant with a fortune would pay for. The middle class liked some show for its money; but again it was the ostentation without the vulgarity of wealth. Looking upon his beautiful house, or worshipping beside his family tombs, with the merchant's mark on the brasses, in St. Katherine's aisle, Thomas Paycocke must often have blessed the noble industry which supported him.

The wills of the Paycockes tell the same story. To whom beside his family does Thomas leave legacies but the good folk of the neighbourhood, who worked for him. There is the Goodday family of cheerful name, two of whom were shearmen, or cloth finishers, and had substantial gifts. "I bequeath to Thomas Goodday Sherman xx s. and ych of his childryn iij s. iiij d. apece. Item, I bequeth to Edward Goodday Sherman xvj s. viij d., and to his child iij s. iiij d." He also left money to Robert Goodday of Sampford and to Robert's brother John, and to each of Robert's sisters, with something extra for Grace, who was his goddaughter; and he did not forget Nicholas Goodday of Stisted and Robert Goodday of Coggeshall and their families, nor their relative John, who was a priest and had ten shillings for a trental. All these Gooddays were doubtless bound to Thomas Paycocke by ties of work as well as of friendship. They belonged to a well-known Coggeshall family, for generations connected with the cloth industry. Thomas Paycocke's namesake and grand-nephew, whose will is dated 1580, was still in close relations with them, and left "to Edwarde Goodaye my godson Fourtie shillinges and to every brother and sister the saide Edwarde hath livinge at the tyme of my decease tenne shillinges a pece," and "unto William Gooday thelder tenne shillinges." The hurrying, scattering generation of to-day can hardly imagine the immovable stability of the village of past centuries, when generation after generation grew from cradle to grave in the same houses, on the same cobbled streets, and folk of the same name were still friends, as their fathers and grandfathers had been before them.

Other friends and employees of Thomas Paycocke also had their legacies. He leaves 6s. 8d. to Humphrey Stonor, "somtyme my prentis." We may see Humphrey Stonor, with sleepy eyes, making his way downstairs on a frosty morning, from those huge raftered attics, where perhaps the 'prentices used to sleep. He was on terms of impudent friendship, no doubt, with the weavers and fullers whom his master set to work; withal a young man of good family, a relative perchance of those Stonors for whom Thomas Betson worked, for, as Deloney wrote, "the yonger sons of knights and gentlemen, to whom their Fathers would leave no lands, were most commonly preferred to learn this trade, to the end that thereby they might live in good estate and drive forth their days in prosperity." Two of his friends got substantial legacies; apparently Thomas Paycocke had lent them money and wished to wipe out the debt upon his death-bed, for, says the will, "I bequethe to John Beycham, my weyver, v li and [i.e. if] there be so moch bitwene vs and ells to mak it vp v li, and a gowne and a doublett. . . . I bequeth and forgive Robert Taylor, fuller, all that is betwixt vs, and more I give him iij s. iiij d." Other legacies show even more clearly that his operations were on a larger scale. "I bequeth to all my wevers, ffullers and shermen that be not afore Rehersed by name xij d. apece, And will they that have wrought me verey moch wark have iij s. iiij d. apece. Item, I bequeth to be distributed amonge my Kembers, Carders and Spynners summa iiij li." [5] Here are all the branches of the cloth industry at a glance. It is Thomas Paycocke, clothier, round whom the whole manufacture revolves. He gives the wool to the women to comb it and card it and spin it; he receives it from them again and gives it to the weaver to be woven into cloth; he gives the cloth to the fuller to be fulled and the dyer to be dyed; and having received it when finished, he has it made up into dozens and sends it off to the wholesale dealer, the draper, who sells it; perhaps he has been wont to send it to that very "Thomas Perpoint, draper," whom he calls "my cosyn" and makes his executor. The whole of

Thomas Paycocke's daily business is implicit in his will. In the year of his death he was still employing a large number of workers and was on friendly and benevolent terms with them. The building of his house had not signalized his retirement from business, as happened when another great clothier, Thomas Dolman, gave up cloth-making and the weavers of Newbury went about lamenting:

> Lord have mercy upon us, miserable sinners.
> Thomas Dolman has built a new house and turned away
> all his spinners.[6]

The relations between Paycocke and his employees evinced in his will are happy ones. Such was not always the case, for if the clothiers of this age had some of the virtues of capitalists, they also had many of their vices, and the age-old strife of capital and labour was already well advanced in the fifteenth century. One detail Paycocke's will does not give us, which we should be glad to know: did he employ only domestic weavers, working in their own houses, or did he also keep a certain number of looms working in his house? It was characteristic of the period in which he lived that something like a miniature factory system was establishing itself in the midst of the new outwork system. The clothiers were beginning to set up looms in their own houses and to work them by journeymen weavers; as a rule the independent weavers greatly disliked the practice, for either they were forced from the position of free masters into that of hired servants, obliged to go and work in the clothier's loom shop, or else they found their payment forced down by the competition of the journeymen. Moreover, the clothiers sometimes owned and let out looms to their work-people, and then also part of the industrial independence of the weaver was lost. All through the first half of the sixteenth century the weavers in the cloth districts kept on petitioning Parliament against this new evil of capitalism. It was as though, long before it established itself in England, they had a prevision of the factory system and of the worker no longer owning either his raw material, his tool, his workshop, or the produce of his industry, but only his labour; the master-weaver dwindled to a hired hand. Certainly the practice was growing in Essex, where, some twenty years after Thomas Paycocke's death, the weavers petitioned against the clothiers, who had their own looms and weavers and fullers in their own houses, so that the petitioners were rendered destitute; "for the rich men, the clothiers, be concluded and agreed among themselves to hold and pay one price for weaving the said cloths," a price too small to support their households, even if they worked day and night, holiday and work-day, so that many of them lost their independence and were reduced to become other men's servants." [7] Nevertheless, the out-work system remained the more common, and without doubt the majority of Paycocke's workers lived in their own cottages, though it is probable also that he had some looms in his house, perhaps in the long, low room at the back, which is traditionally supposed to have been used for weaving, perhaps in a shed or "spinning house."

A highly idyllic picture of work in one of these miniature factories, which we may amuse ourselves by applying to Thomas Paycocke's, is contained in Deloney's *Pleasant History of Jack of Newbery*. Jack of Newbury was an historical character, a very famous clothier named John Winchcomb who died at Newbury only a year later than Paycocke himself, and of whom Paycocke must certainly have heard, for his kersies were famous on the Continent, and old Fuller, who celebrates him among his *Worthies of England* calls him "the most considerable clothier (without fancy or fiction) England ever beheld." [8] The tales of how he had led a hundred of his own 'prentices to Flodden Field, how he had feasted the King and Queen in his house at Newbury, how he had built part of Newbury Church, and how he had refused a knighthood, preferring "to rest in his russet coat a poor clothier to his dying day," spread about England, growing as they spread. In 1597 Thomas Deloney, the forefather of the novel, enshrined them in a rambling tale, half prose and half verse, which soon became extremely popular. It is from this tale that we may take an imaginary picture of work in a clothier's house, being wary to remember, however, that it is an exaggeration, a legend, and that the great John Winchcomb certainly never had as many as two hundred looms in his own house, while our Thomas Paycocke probably had not more than a dozen. But the poet must have his licence, for, after all, the spirit of the ballad is the thing, and it is always a pleasant diversion to drop into rhyme:

> Within one roome, being large and long
> There stood two hundred Loomes full strong.
> Two hundred men, the truth is so,
> Wrought in these Loomes all in a row.
> By every one a pretty boy
> Sate making quilts with mickle joy,
> And in another place hard by
> A hundred women merily
> Were carding hard with joyfull cheere
> Who singing sate with voyces cleere,
> And in a chamber close beside
> Two hundred maidens did abide,
> In petticoats of Stammell red,
> And milk white kerchers on their head.
> Their smocke-sleeves like to winter snow
> That on the Westerne mountaines flow,
> And each sleeve with a silken band
> Was featly tied at the hand.
> These pretty maids did never lin
> But in that place all day did spin,
> And spinning so with voyces meet
> Like nightingales they sang full sweet.
> Then to another roome came they
> Where children were in poore aray;
> And every one sate picking wool
> The finest from the course to cull:
> The number was sevenscore and ten
> The children of poore silly men:
> And these their labours to requite
> Had every one a penny at night,
> Beside their meat and drinke all day,
> Which was to them a wondrous stay.
> Within another place likewise

Full fifty proper men he spies
And these were sheremen everyone,
Whose skill and cunning there was showne:
And hard by them there did remaine
Full four-score rowers taking paine
A Dye-house likewise had he then,
Wherein he kept full forty men:
And likewise in his Fulling Mill
Full twenty persons kept he still.
Each weeke ten good fat oxen he
Spent in his house for certaintie,
Beside good butter, cheese and fish
And many another wholesome dish.
He kept a Butcher all the yeere,
A Brewer eke for Ale and Beere;
A Baker for to bake his Bread,
Which stood his hushold in good stead.
Five Cookes within his kitchin great
Were all the yeare to dress his meat.
Six Scullion boyes vnto their hands,
To make clean dishes, pots and pans,
Beside poore children that did stay
To turne the broaches every day.
The old man that did see this sight
Was much amaz'd, as well he might:
This was a gallant Cloathier sure,
Whose fame forever shall endure.[9]

The private life of Thomas Paycocke, no less than his business, can be made to live again. Of his family the invaluable
will tells us a little. His first wife was that Margaret whose
initials, together with his own, decorate the woodwork of the
house, and indeed it is probable that old John Paycocke built
the house for the young couple on their wedding. Gay, indeed,
must have been the sights which it witnessed on that happy
day, for our ancestors knew how to put their hearts into a wedding, and Merry England was never merrier than when the

bridegroom led home the bride. We may borrow once again from Deloney's idyll, to recreate the scene:

The Bride being attyred in a gowne of sheepes russet and a kertle of fine woosted, her head attyred with a billiment of gold and her haire as yeallow as gold hanging downe behinde her, which was curiously combed and pleated, according to the manner in those dayes; shee was led to Church betweene two sweete boyes, with Bridelaces and Rosemary tied about their silken sleeves. Then was there a fair Bride-cup of silver and gilt carried before her, wherein was a goodly branch of Rosemary gilded very faire, hung about with silken Ribands of all colours; next was there a noyse of Musicians that played all the way before her; after her came all the chiefest maydens of the Country, some bearing great Bride Cakes and some Garlands of wheate finely gilded and so she past unto the Church. It is needlesse for mee to make any mention here of the Bridegroome, who being a man so well beloued, wanted no company and those of the best sort, beside diuers Marchant strangers of the Stillyard that came from London to the wedding. The marriage being solemnized, home they came in order as before and to dinner they went where was no want of good cheare, no lack of melody. . . . The wedding endured ten dayes, to the great reliefe of the poore that dwelt all about.[10]

Much dancing the house doubtless saw under the beautiful carved roof of the hall, with much song, games, kissing, and general abandon. Even when the bride and groom retired to the bridal chamber with its roll-moulded beams the merry-making was not done; they must hold a levee to their nearest friends in the bed-chamber itself, enthroned in the great four-poster bed. There was no false delicacy about our ancestors. Indeed, as Henry Bullinger says (he was a very different person from jovial Deloney, but he was a contemporary of Paycocke's, and Coverdale translated him, so let him speak): "After supper must they begynne to pype and daunce agayne of the new. And though the yonge parsones, beynge weery of the bablyng noyse and inconuenience, come ones towarde theyer

rest, yet can they haue no quietnesse. For a man shall fynd un-
manerly and restlesse people, that will first go to theyr chambre
dore, and there syng vycious and naughtie balates that the
deuell maye haue his triumphe now to the vttermost." [11]
What would we not give for one of those "naughty ballads"
to-day?

The bride Margaret, who was somewhat after this merry
fashion brought home to Coggeshall, came from Clare, the
ancient home of the Coggeshall Paycockes. She was the daughter of one Thomas Horrold, for whose memory Paycocke re-
tained a lively affection and respect, for in founding a chantry
in Coggeshall Church he desired specially that it should be
for the souls of himself and his wife, his mother and father, and
his father-in-law, Thomas Horrold of Clare. He also left five
pounds, with which his executors were "to purvey an oder
stone to be hade to Clare chirch and layd on my ffader in lawe
Thomas Horrold w^t his pycture and his wife and childryn
theron" (i.e. a memorial brass), and also five cows or else
three pounds in money to Clare Church "to kepe and mayn-
tene my ffader in lawe Thomas Horrold his obitt." He also
left money to his wife's brother and sisters. Margaret Paycocke died before her husband and without children; and the
only young folk of his name whom Thomas ever saw at play
in his lofty hall, or climbing upon his dresser to find the head,
as small as a walnut, hidden in the carving of the ceiling, were
his nephews and nieces, Robert and Margaret Uppcher, his
sister's children; John, the son of his brother John; and Thomas,
Robert, and Emma, the children of his brother Robert; perhaps also his little godchild Grace Goodday. It was perhaps in
the hope of a son to whom he might leave his house and name
that Thomas Paycocke married again a girl called Ann Cotton.
She was the wife of his old age, "Anne my good wif," and her
presence must have made bright the beautiful house, silent and
lonely since Margaret died. Her father, George Cotton, is
mentioned in the will, and her brothers and sister, Richard,
William, and Eleanor, have substantial legacies. But Thomas
and Ann enjoyed only a short term of married life; she brought
him his only child, but death overtook him before it was born.

In his will he provides carefully for Ann; she is to have five hundred marks sterling, and as long as she lives the beautiful house is to be hers; for to his elaborate arrangements for its inheritance he adds, "provided alwey that my wif Ann haue my house that I dwell in while she lyvyth at hir pleyser and my dof house [dove-house] with the garden y^t stoundeth in." A gap in the Paycocke records makes it difficult to say whether Thomas Paycocke's child lived or died; but it seems probable that it either died or was a girl, for Paycocke had bequeathed the house, provided that he had no male heirs, to his nephew John (son of his eldest brother John), and in 1575 we find it in the hands of this John Paycocke, while the house next door was in the hands of another Thomas Paycocke, his brother Robert's son. This Thomas died about 1580, leaving only daughters, and after him, in 1584, died John Paycocke, sadly commemorated in the parish register as "the last of his name in Coxall." So the beautiful house passed out of the hands of the great family of clothiers who had held it for nearly a hundred years.[12]

Of Thomas Paycocke's personal character it is also possible to divine something from his will. He was obviously a kind and benevolent employer, as his thought for his work-people and their children shows. He was often asked to stand godfather to the babies of Coggeshall, for in his will he directs that at his burial and the ceremonies which were repeated on the seventh day and "month mind" after it there were to be "xxiiij or xij smale childryn in Rochettes with tapers in theire hands and as many as may be of them lett them be my god childryn and they to have vj s. viij d. apece and euery oder child iiij d. apece . . . and also euery god chyld besyde vj s. viij d. apece." All these children were probably little bread-winners, employed at a very early age in sorting Thomas Paycocke's wool. "Poore people," says Thomas Deloney, "whom God lightly blessed with most children, did by meanes of this occupation so order them, that by the time they were come to be sixe or seven yeeres of age, they were able to get their owne bread";[13] and when Defoe rode from Blackstone Edge to Halifax, observing the cloth manufacture, which occupied all the villages of the

West Riding, it was one of his chief grounds for admiration that "all [were] employed, from the youngest to the oldest; scarce any thing above four years old, but its hands were sufficient for its own support." [14] The employment of children at what we should regard as an excessively early age was by no means a new phenomenon introduced with the Industrial Revolution.

That Thomas Paycocke had many friends, not only in Coggeshall but in the villages round, the number of his legacies bears witness. His will also shows that he was a man of deep religious feeling. He was a brother of the Crutched Friars of Colchester and left them on his death five pounds to pray "for me and for them that I am bound to pray fore." It was customary in the Middle Ages for monastic houses to give the privilege of the fraternity of the house to benefactors and persons of distinction; the reception took place at a long and elaborate ceremony, during which the *confrater* received the kiss of peace from all the brethren. It is a mark of the respect in which Thomas Paycocke was held in the countryside that he should have been made a brother by the Crutched Friars. He seems to have had a special kindness for the Order of Friars; he left the Grey Friars of Colchester and the Friars of Maldon, Chelmsford, and Sudbury each ten shillings for a trental and 3s. 4d. to repair their houses; and to the Friars of Clare he left twenty shillings for two trentals, "and at Lent after my deceste a kade of Red heryng." He had great interest in Coggeshall Abbey; it lay less than a mile from his house, and he must often have dined in state with the abbot at his guest table on feast days and attended Mass in the abbey church. He remembered the abbey as he lay dying, and the sound of its bells ringing for vespers came softly in at his window on the mellow September air; and he left "my Lord Abbot and Convent" one of his famous broadcloths and four pounds in money "for to have a dirige and Masse and their belles Ryngyng at my buriall when it is doon at Chirche, lyke-wyse the vij[th] day and mounth day, with iij tryntalls upon the same day yf they can serve them, orells when they can at more leasur, Summa x li."

His piety is shown also in his bequests to the churches of Bradwell, Pattiswick, and Markshall, parishes adjacent to Coggeshall, and to Stoke Naylond, Clare, Poslingford, Ovington, and Beauchamp St. Pauls, over the Essex border, in the district from which the Paycockes originally came. But his greatest care was naturally for Coggeshall Church. One of the Paycockes had probably built the north aisle, where the altar was dedicated to St. Katherine, and all the Paycocke tombs lay there. Thomas Paycocke left instructions in his will that he should be buried before St. Katherine's altar, and made the following gifts to the church: "Item, I bequeth to the high aulter of Coxhall Chirche in recompence of tithes and all oder thyngs forgoten Summa iiij li. Item, I bequethe to the Tabernacle of the Trenyte at the high awlter and an other of Seint Margarete in seint Katryne Ile, there as the greate Lady stands, for carvyng and gildyng of them summa c. marcs sterlinge. Item, to the reparacons of the Chirch and bells and for my lying in the Chirche summa c. nobles." He founded a chantry there also and left money to be given weekly to six poor men to attend Mass in his chantry thrice a week.

Of piety and of family pride these legacies to religious houses and to churches speak clearly. Another series of legacies, which takes a form characteristic of medieval charity, bears witness perhaps to Thomas Paycocke's habits. He must often have ridden abroad, to see the folk who worked for him or to visit his friends in the villages round Coggeshall; or farther afield to Clare, first to see the home of his ancestors, then to court Margaret Horrold, his bride, and then, with Margaret beside him, to visit his well-loved father-in-law. Certainly, whether he walked to church in Coggeshall, or whether he rode along the country lanes, he often sighed over the state of the road as he went; often he must have struggled through torrents of mud in winter or stumbled among holes in summer; for in the Middle Ages the care of the roads was a matter for private or ecclesiastical charity, and all except the great highways were likely to be but indifferently kept. Langland, in his *Piers Plowman*, mentions the amending of "wikked wayes" (by which he means not bad habits but bad roads) as one of those works of charity which rich merchants must do for the salvation of their souls. Thomas Paycocke's choice of roads no doubt reflects many a wearisome journey, from which he returned home splashed and testy, to the ministrations of "John Reyner my man" or "Henry Briggs my servant," and of Margaret, looking anxiously from her oriel window for his return. In his own town he leaves no less than forty pounds, of which twenty pounds was to go to amend a section of West Street (where his house stood), and the other twenty was "to be layde on the fowle wayes bitwene Coxhall and Blackwater where as moost nede ys"; he had doubtless experienced the evils of this road on his way to the abbey. Farther afield, he leaves twenty pounds for the "fowle way" between Clare and Ovington, and another twenty for the road between Ovington and Beauchamp St. Pauls.

As his life drew to its close he doubtless rode less often afield. The days would pass peacefully for him; his business flourished and he was everywhere loved and respected. He took pride in his lovely house, adding bit by bit to its beauties. In the cool of the evening he must often have stood outside the garden room and seen the monks from the big abbey fishing in their stewpond across the field, or lifted his eyes to where the last rays of sun slanted on to the lichened roof of the great tithe-barn, and on to the rows of tenants, carrying their sheaves of corn along the road; and he reflected, perhaps, that John Mann and Thomas Spooner, his own tenants, were good, steady friends, and that it were well to leave them a gown or a pound when he died. Often also, in his last year or two, he must have sat with his wife in his garden with the dove-house and watched the white pigeons circling round the apple-trees, and smiled upon her bed of flowers. And in winter evenings sometimes he would take his furred cloak and stroll to the Dragon Inn, and Edward Aylward, mine host, would welcome him with bows; and so he would sit and drink a tankard of sack with his neighbours, very slow and dignified, as befitted the greatest clothier of the town, and looking benevolently upon the company. But at times he would frown, if he saw a truant monk from the abbey stolen out for a drink in spite of all the prohibitions of bishop and abbot, shaking his head, perhaps, and complaining that religion was not what it had been in the good old days; but not meaning much of it, as his will shows, and never dreaming that twenty years after his death abbot and monks would be scattered and the King's servants would be selling at auction the lead from off the roof of Coggeshall Abbey; never dreaming that after four hundred years his house would still stand, mellow and lovely, with its carved ceiling and its proud merchant's mark, when the abbey church was only a shadow on the surface of a field in hot weather and all the abbey buildings were shrunk to one ruined ambulatory, ignobly sheltering blue Essex hay wagons from the rain.

So Thomas Paycocke's days drew to a close amid the peace and beauty of the most English of counties, "fatt, frutefull and full of profitable thinges," [15] whose little rolling hills, wych elms, and huge clouded skies Constable loved to paint. There came a day of September when gloom hung over the streets of Coggeshall, when the spinning-wheels were silent in the cottages, and spinners and weavers stood in anxious groups outside the beautiful house in West Street; for upstairs in his bridal chamber, under its noble ceiling, the great clothier lay dying, and his wife wept by his bedside, knowing that he would never see his child. A few days later the cottages were deserted again, and a concourse of weeping people followed Thomas Paycocke to his last rest. The ceremony of his burial befitted his dignity: it comprised services, not only on burial day itself, but on the seventh day after it, and then again after a month had passed. It is given best in the words of his will, for Thomas Paycocke followed the custom of his time, in giving his executors elaborate injunctions for his funeral rites: "I will myne executors bestowe vpon my buryng daye, vij day and mounthe daye after this manner: At my buriall to have a tryntall of prests and to be at dirige, lawdis and comendacons as many of them as may be purveyed that day to scrve the tryntall, and yf eny lack to make it vpp the vij[th] daye. And at the Mounthe daye an oder tryntall to be purveyed hoole of myne executors and to kepe dirige, lawdis and commendacons as is afore reherssed, with iij high massis be note [by note, i.e. with music], oon of the

holy gost, an other of owre lady, and an other of Requiem, both
buriall, seuenth day and Mounthe daye. And prests beyng at
this obseruance iiij d. at euery tyme and childryn at euery
tyme ij d., w^t torches at the buriall xij, and vj at the vijth day
and xij at the mounthe daye, with xxiij^{ti} or xij smale childryn
in Rochettes with tapers in theire honds, and as many as may
be of them lett them be my god Childryn, and they to haue vj s.
viij d. apece; and euery oder child iiij d. apece; and euery man
that holdith torches at euery day he to have ij apece; and euery
man woman and child that holdeth upp hound [hand] at eny of
thes iij days to haue j d. apece; And also euery god chyld besyde vj s. viij d. apece; and to the Ryngars for all iij dayes x s.;
and for mete, drynke, and for twoo Semones of a doctor, and
also to haue a dirige at home, or I be borne to the Chirche
summa j li."

Here is something very different from the modest Thomas
Betson's injunction: "The costes of my burying to be don not
outrageously, but sobrely and discretly and in a meane maner,
that it may be unto the worship and laude of Almyghty God."
The worthy old clothier was not unmindful of the worship
and laud of Thomas Paycocke also, and over £500 in modern
money was expended upon his burial ceremonies, over and
above the cost of founding his new chantry. Well indeed it
was that his eyes were closed in death, ere the coming of the
Reformation abolished all the chantries of England, and with
them the Paycocke chantry in St. Katherine's aisle, which had
provided alms for six poor men weekly. Thomas Paycocke belonged to the good old days; in a quarter of a century after his
death Essex was already changing. The monks were scattered
from the abbey, which stood roofless; the sonorous Latin
tongue no longer echoed in the church, nor priests prayed there
for the souls of Thomas and his wife and his parents and
his father-in-law. Even the cloth industry was changing, and
the county was growing more prosperous still with the advent
of finer kinds of cloth, brought over there by feat-fingered
aliens, the "new drapery," known as "Bays and Says." For as
the adage says:

> Hops, reformation, bays and beer
> Came into England all in a year,

and Coggeshall was destined to become more famous still for a new sort of cloth called "Coxall's Whites," which Thomas Paycocke's nephews made when he was in his grave.[16] One thing, however, did not change; for his beautiful house still stood in West Street, opposite the vicarage, and was the delight of all who saw it. It stands there still, and looking upon it to-day, and thinking of Thomas Paycocke who once dwelt in it, do there not come to mind the famous words of Ecclesiasticus?

"Let us now praise famous men and our fathers that begat us.

The Lord hath wrought great glory by them through His great power from the beginning. . . .

Rich men furnished with ability, living peaceably in their habitations:

All these were honoured in their generations and were the glory of their times."

CHAPTER I

THE PEASANT BODO

A. RAW MATERIAL

1. The Roll of the Abbot Irminon, an estate book of the Abbey of St. Germain des Prés, near Paris, written between 811 and 826. See *Polyptyque de l'Abbaye de Saint-Germain des Prés*, pub. Auguste Longnon, t. I, *Introduction*; t. II, *Texte* (Soc. de l'Hist. de Paris, 1886–95).

2. Charlemagne's capitulary, *De Villis*, instructions to his stewards on the management of his estates. See Guerard, *Explication du Capitulaire "de Villis"* (Acad. des Inscriptions et Belles-Lettres, *Mémoires*, t. XXI, 1857), pp. 165–309, containing the text, with a detailed commentary and a translation into French.

3. *Early Lives of Charlemagne*, ed. A. J. Grant (King's Classics, 1907). Contains the lives by Einhard and the Monk of St. Gall, on which see Halphen, cited below.

4. Various pieces of information about social life may be gleaned from the decrees of Church Councils, Old High German and Anglo-Saxon charms and poems, and Ælfric's *Colloquium*, extracts from which are translated in Bell's Eng. Hist. Source Books, *The Welding of the Race*, 449–1066, ed. J. E. W. Wallis (1913). For a general sketch of the period see Lavisse *Hist. de France*, t. II, and for an elaborate critical study of certain aspects of Charlemagne's reign (including the *Polyptychum*) see Halphen, *Études critiques sur l'Histoire de Charlemagne* (1921); also A. Dopsch, *Wirtschaftsentwicklung der Karolingerzeit, Vornehmlich in Deutschland*, 2 vols. (Weimar, 1912–13), which Halphan criticizes.

B. NOTES TO THE TEXT

[1] "Habet Bodo colonus et uxor ejus colona, nomine Ermen-

trudis, homines sancti Germani, habent secum infantes III.
Tenet mansum ingenuilem I, habentem de terre arabili
bunuaria VIII et antsingas II, de vinea aripennos II, de prato
aripennos VII. Solvit ad hostem de argento solidos II, de
vino in pascione modios II; ad tertium annum sundolas C;
de sepe perticas III. Arat ad hibernaticum perticas III, ad
tramisem perticas II. In unaquaque ebdomada corvadas II,
manuoperam I. Pullos III, ova XV; et caropera ibi injungitur.
Et habet medietatem de farinarium, inde solvit de argento
solidos II." Op. cit., II, p. 78. "Bodo a colonus and his wife
Ermentrude a colona, tenants of Saint-Germain, have with
them three children. He holds one free manse, containing eight
bunuaria and two antsinga of arable land two aripenni of
vines and seven aripenni of meadow. He pays two silver shillings to the army and two hogsheads of wine for the right to
pasture his pigs in the woods. Every third year he pays a hundred planks and three poles for fences. He ploughs at the
winter sowing four perches and at the spring sowing two
perches. Every week he owes two labour services (corvees) and
one handwork. He pays three fowls and fifteen eggs, and carrying service when it is enjoined upon him. And he owns the
half of a windmill, for which he pays two silver shillings."

² De Villis, c. 45.

³ Ibid. cc. 43, 49.

⁴ From "The Casuistry of Roman Meals," in The Collected
Writings of Thomas De Quincey, ed. D. Masson (1897), VII,
p. 13.

⁵ Ælfric's Colloquium in op. cit. p. 95.

⁶ The Monk of St. Gall's Life in Early Lives of Charlemagne, pp. 87–8.

⁷ Einhard's Life in op. cit., p. 45.

⁸ Anglo-Saxon charms translated in Stopford Brook, English
Literature from the Beginning to the Norman Conquest
(1899), p. 43.

[9] Old High German charm written in a tenth-century hand in a ninth-century codex containing sermons of St. Augustine, now in the Vatican Library. Brawne, *Althochdeutsches Lesebuch* (fifth edition, Halle, 1902), p. 83.

[10] Another Old High German charm preserved in a tenth-century codex now at Vienna. Brawne, *op. cit.*, p. 164.

[11] From the ninth-century *Libellus de Ecclesiasticis Disciplinis*, art. 100, quoted in Ozanam, *La Civilisation Chrétienne chez les Francs* (1849), p. 312. The injunction, however, really refers to the recently conquered and still half-pagan Saxons.

[12] *Penitential* of Halitgart, Bishop of Cambrai, quoted *ibid.* p. 314.

[13] *Documents relatifs à l'Histoire de l'Industrie et du Commerce en France*, ed. G. Faigniez, t. I, pp. 51–2.

[14] See references in Chambers, *The Medieval Stage* (1913), I, pp. 161–3.

[15] For the famous legend of the dancers of Kölbigk, see Gaston Paris, *Les Danseurs Maudits, Légende Allemande du XIe Siècle* (Paris 1900, reprinted from the *Journal des Savants*, Dec., 1899), which is a *conte rendu* of Schröder's study in *Zeitschrift für Kirchengeschichte* (1899). The poem occurs in a version of English origin, in which one of the dancers, Thierry, is cured of a perpetual trembling in all his limbs by a miracle of St. Edith at the nunnery of Wilton in 1065. See *loc. cit.*, pp. 10, 14.

[16] "Swete Lamman dhin are," in the original. The story is told by Giraldus Cambrensis in *Gemma Ecclesiastica*, pt. I, c. XLII. See *Selections from Giraldus Cambrensis*, ed. C. A. J. Skeel (S.P.C.K. *Texts for Students*, No. XI), p. 48.

[17] Einhard's *Life* in *op. cit.* p. 45. See also *ibid.*, p. 168 (note).

[18] The Monk of St. Gall's *Life* in *op. cit.*, pp. 144–7.

[19] Einhard's *Life* in *op. cit.*, p. 39.

[20] *Ibid.*, p. 35.

[21] Beazley, *Dawn of Modern Geography* (1897), I, p. 325.

[22] The Monk of St. Gall's *Life* in *op. cit.*, pp. 78–9.

[23] See the description in Lavisse, *Hist. de France* II, pt. I, p. 321; also G. Monod, *Les mœurs judiciaires au VIIIe Siècle*, Revue Historique, t. XXXV (1887).

[24] See Faigniez, *op. cit.*, pp. 43–4.

[25] See the Monk of St. Gall's account of the finery of the Frankish nobles: "It was a holiday and they had just come from Pavia, whither the Venetians had carried all the wealth of the East from their territories beyond the sea,—others, I say, strutted in robes made of pheasant-skins and silk; or of the necks, backs and tails of peacocks in their first plumage. Some were decorated with purple and lemon-coloured ribbons; some were wrapped round with blankets and some in ermine robes." *Op. cit.*, p. 149. The translation is a little loose: the "phœnix robes" of the original were more probably made out of the plumage, not of the pheasant but of the scarlet flamingo, as Hodgson thinks (*Early Hist. of Venice*, p. 155), or possibly silks woven or embroidered with figures of birds, as Heyd thinks (*Hist. du Commerce du Levant*, I, p. 111).

[26] The Monk of St. Gall's *Life* in *op. cit.*, pp. 81–2.

[27] This little poem was scribbled by an Irish scribe in the margin of a copy of Priscian in the monastery of St. Gall, in Switzerland, the same from which Charlemagne's highly imaginative biographer came. The original will be found in Stokes and Strachan, *Thesaurus Palæohibernicus* (1903) II, p. 290. It has often been translated and I quote the translation by Kuno Meyer, *Ancient Irish Poetry* (2nd ed., 1913), p. 99. The quotation from the *Triads of Ireland* at the head of this chapter is taken from Kuno Meyer also, *ibid.* pp. 102–3.

CHAPTER II

MARCO POLO

A. Raw Material

1. *The Book of Ser Marco Polo the Venetian concerning the Kingdoms and Marvels of the East,* trans. and ed. with notes by Sir Henry Yule (3rd edit., revised by Henri Cordier, 2 vols., Hakluyt Soc., 1903). See also H. Cordier, *Ser Marco Polo: Notes and Addenda* (1920). The best edition of the original French text is *Le Livre de Marco Polo,* ed. G. Pauthier (Paris, 1865). The most convenient and cheap edition of the book for English readers is a reprint of Marsden's translation (of the Latin text) and notes (first published, 1818), with an introduction by John Masefield, *The Travels of Marco Polo the Venetian* (Everyman's Library, 1908; reprinted, 1911); but some of the notes (identifying places, etc.) are now out of date, and the great edition by Yule and Cordier should be consulted where exact and detailed information is required. It is a mine of information, geographical and historical, about the East. I quote from the Everyman Edition as Marco Polo, *op. cit.,* and from the Yule edition as Yule, *op. cit.*

2. *La Cronique des Veneciens de Maistre Martin da Canal.* In *Archivo Storico Italiano,* 1st ser., vol. VIII (Florence, 1845). Written in French and accompanied by a translation into modern Italian. One of the most charming of medieval chronicles.

B. Modern Works

1. For medieval Venice see—
   F. C. Hodgson: *The Early History of Venice from the Foundation to the Conquest of Constantinople* (1901); and *Venice in the Thirteenth and Fourteenth Centuries, A Sketch of Venetian History,* 1204–1400 (1910).
   P. G. Molmenti: *Venice, its Growth to the Fall of the*

Republic, vols. I and II (*The Middle Ages*), trans. H. F. Brown (1906); and *La Vie Privée à Venise*, vol. I (1895).

H. F. Brown: *Studies in the History of Venice*, vol. I (1907).

Mrs. Oliphant: *The Makers of Venice* (1905) is pleasant reading and contains a chapter on Marco Polo.

2. For medieval China, the Tartars, and European intercourse with the far East see—

Sir Henry Yule's introduction to his great edition of Marco Polo (above).

Cathay and the Way Thither: *Medieval Notices of China*, trans. and ed. by Sir Henry Yule, 4 vols. (Hakluyt Soc., 1915–6). Contains an invaluable introduction and all the best accounts of China left by medieval European travellers. Above all, Oderic of Pordenone (*d.* 1331) should be read as a pendant to Marco Polo.

R. Beazley: *The Dawn of Modern Geography*, vols. II and III (1897–1906).

R. Grousset: *Histoire de l'Asie*, t. III (3rd edit., 1922), Chap. I. A short and charmingly written account of the Mongol Empires from Genghis Khan to Timour.

H. Howarth: *History of the Mongols* (1876). A new edition is announced to appear shortly.

3. For medieval trade with the East the best book is—

W. Heyd: *Histoire du Commerce du Levant au Moyen-Âge*, trans., F. Raynaud; 2 vols. (Leipzig and Paris, 1885–6, reprinted 1923).

C. Notes to the Text

[1] To be exact, the Flanders galleys which sailed via Gibraltar to Southampton and Bruges were first sent out forty years after 1268—in 1308. Throughout the fourteenth and fifteenth centuries they sailed every year, and Southampton owes its rise to prosperity to the fact that it was their port of call.

[2] The occasion of the speech quoted was when the imperial representative Longinus was trying to get the help of the Venetians against the Lombards in 568 and invited them to acknowledge themselves subjects of the Emperor. The speech is quoted in *Encyclop. Brit.*, Art. *Venice* (by H. F. Brown), p. 1002. The episode of the loaves of bread belongs to the attempt of Pipin, son of Charlemagne, to starve out the Rialto in the winter of 809–10. Compare the tale of Charlemagne casting his sword into the sea, with the words, "Truly, even as this brand which I have cast into the sea shall belong neither to me nor to you nor to any other man in all the world, even so shall no man in the world have power to hurt the realm of Venice; and he who would harm it shall feel the wrath and displeasure of God, even as it has fallen upon me and my people."—See Canale, *Cron.*, c. VIII. These are, of course, all legends.

[3] "Voirs est que la mer Arians est de le ducat de Venise." —Canale, *op. cit.*, p. 600. Albertino Mussato calls Venice "dominatrix Adriaci maris."—Molmenti, *Venice*, I, p. 120.

[4] See some good contemporary accounts of the ceremony quoted in Molmenti, *Venice*, I, pp. 212–15.

[5] During the fatal war of Chioggia between the two republics of Venice and Genoa, which ended in 1381, it was said that the Genoese admiral (or some say Francesco Carrara), when asked by the Doge to receive peace ambassadors, replied, "Not before I have bitted the horses on St. Mark's."—H. F. Brown, *Studies in the Hist. of Venice*, I, p. 130.

[6] Canale, *op. cit.*, p. 270.

[7] "The weather was clear and fine . . . and when they were at sea, the mariners let out the sails to the wind, and let the ships run with spread sails before the wind over the sea"—See, for instance. Canale, *op. cit.*, pp. 320, 326, and elsewhere.

⁸ Canale, *op. cit.*, cc. I and II, pp. 268–72. Venice is particularly fortunate in the descriptions which contemporaries have left of her—not only her own citizens (such as Canale, Sanudo and the Doge Mocenigo) but also strangers. Petrarch's famous description of Venetian commerce, as occasioned by the view which he saw from his window in the fourteenth century, has often been quoted: "See the innumerable vessels which set forth from the Italian shore in the desolate winter, in the most variable and stormy spring, one turning its prow to the east, the other to the west; some carrying our wine to foam in British cups, our fruits to flatter the palates of the Scythians and, still more hard of credence, the wood of our forests to the Egean and the Achaian isles; some to Syria, to Armenia, to the Arabs and Persians, carrying oil and linen and saffron, and bringing back all their diverse goods to us. . . . Let me persuade you to pass another hour in my company. It was the depth of night and the heavens were full of storm, and I, already weary and half asleep, had come to an end of my writing, when suddenly a burst of shouts from the sailors penetrated my ear. Aware of what these shouts should mean from former experience, I rose hastily and went up to the higher windows of this house, which look out upon the port. Oh, what a spectacle, mingled with feelings of pity, of wonder, of fear and of delight! Resting on their anchors close to the marble banks which serve as a mole to the vast palace which this free and liberal city has conceded to me for my dwelling, several vessels have passed the winter, exceeding with the height of their masts and spars the two towers which flank my house. The larger of the two was at this moment—though the stars were all hidden by the clouds, the winds shaking the walls, and the roar of the sea filling the air—leaving the quay and setting out upon its voyage. Jason and Hercules would have been stupefied with wonder, and Tiphys, seated at the helm, would have been ashamed of the nothing which won him so much fame. If you had seen it, you would have said it was no ship but a mountain swimming upon the sea, although under the weight of its immense wings a great part of it was hidden in the waves. The end

of the voyage was to be the Don, beyond which nothing can navigate from our seas; but many of those who were on board, when they had reached that point, meant to prosecute their journey, never pausing till they had reached the Ganges or the Caucasus, India and the Eastern Ocean. So far does love of gain stimulate the human mind."—Quoted from Petrarch's *Lettere Senili* in Oliphant, *Makers of Venice* (1905), p. 349; the whole of this charming chapter, "The Guest of Venice," should be read. Another famous description of Venice occurs in a letter written by Pietro Aretino, a guest of Venice during the years 1527 to 1533, to Titian, quoted in E. Hutton, *Pietro Aretino, the Scourge of Princes* (1922), pp. 136–7; compare also his description of the view from his window on another occasion, quoted *ib.*, pp. 131–3. The earliest of all is the famous letter written by Cassiodorus to the Venetians in the sixth century, which is partly translated in Molmenti, *op. cit.*, I, pp. 14–15.

[9] The account of the march of the gilds occupies cc. CCLXIII–CCLXXXIII of Canale's Chronicle, *op. cit.*, pp. 602–26. It has often been quoted.

[10] Canale, *op. cit.*, c. CCLXI, p. 600.

[11] This account of Hangchow is taken partly from Marco Polo, *op. cit.*, bk. II, c. LXVIII: "Of the noble and magnificent city of Kinsai"; and partly from Odoric of Pordenone, *Cathay and the Way Thither*, ed. Yule, pp. 113–20.

[12] Oderic of Pordenone, who was a man before he was a friar, remarks: "The Chinese are comely enough, but colourless, having beards of long straggling hair like mousers, cats I mean. And as for the women, they are the most beautiful in the world." Marco Polo likewise never fails to note when the women of a district are specially lovely, in the same way that that other traveller Arthur Young always notes the looks of the chambermaids at the French inns among the other details of the countryside, and is so much affronted if waited on by a plain girl. Marco Polo gives the palm for beauty to the women of the Province of Timochain (or Damaghan) on

the north-east border of Persia, of which, he says, "The people are in general a handsome race, especially the women, who, in my opinion, are the most beautiful in the world."— Marco Polo, *op. cit.*, p. 73. Of the women of Kinsai he reports thus: "The courtesans are accomplished and are perfect in the arts of blandishment and dalliance, which they accompany with expressions adapted to every description of person, insomuch that strangers who have once tasted of their charms, remain in a state of fascination, and become so enchanted by their meretricious arts, that they can never divest themselves of the impression. Thus intoxicated with sensual pleasures, when they return to their homes they report that they have been in Kin-sai, or the celestial city, and pant for the time when they may be enabled to revisit paradise." Of the respectable ladies, wives of the master craftsmen he likewise says: "They have much beauty and are brought up with languid and delicate habits. The costliness of their dresses, in silks and jewellery, can scarcely be imagined."—*op. cit.*, pp. 296, 297–8.

[13] Yule, *op. cit.*, II, p. 184.

[14] For Prester John see Sir Henry Yule's article "Prester John" in the *Encyclopædia Britannica*, and Lynn Thorndike, *A History of Magic and Experimental Science* (1923), II, pp. 236–45. There is a pleasant popular account in S. Baring Gould, *Popular Myths of the Middle Ages* (1866–8).

[15] For their accounts see *The Journal of William of Rubruck to the Eastern Parts, 1253–5, by himself, with two accounts of the Earlier Journey of John of Pian da Carpine*, trans. and ed. with notes by W. W. Rockhill (Hakluyt Soc., 1900). Rubruck especially is a most delightful person.

[16] This, together with the whole account of the first journey of the elder Polos, the circumstances of the second journey, and of their subsequent return occurs in the first chapter of Marco Polo's book, which is a general introduction, after which he proceeds to describe in order the lands through

which he passed. This autobiographical section is unfortunately all too short.

[17] As a matter of fact, William of Rubruck had seen and described it before him.

[18] For Marco Polo's account of this custom in the province which he calls "Kardandan," see *op. cit.*, p. 250. An illustration of it from an album belonging to the close of the Ming dynasty is reproduced in S. W. Bushell, *Chinese Art* (1910), fig. 134.

[19] Marco Polo, *op. cit.*, pp. 21–2.

[20] A certain *Poh-lo* was, according to the Chinese annals of the Mongol dynasty, appointed superintendent of salt mines at Yangchow shortly after 1282. Professor Parker thinks that he may be identified with our Polo, but M. Cordier disagrees. See E. H. Parker *Some New Facts about Marco Polo's Book* in *Imperial and Asiatic Quarterly Review* (1904), p. 128; and H. Cordier, *Ser Marco Polo*, p. 8. See also Yule, *Marco Polo*, I, Introd., p. 21.

[21] P. Parrenin in *Lett. Edif.*, xxiv, 58, quoted in Yule, *op. cit.*, I, Introd., p. 11.

[22] On Marco Polo's omissions see Yule, *op. cit.*, I, Introd., p. 110.

[23] Marco Polo, *op. cit.*, p. 288.

[24] On Chao Mêng-fu see S. W. Bushell, *Chinese Art* (1910), II, pp. 133–59; H. A. Giles, *Introd. to the History of Chinese Pictorial Art* (Shanghai, 2nd ed., 1918), pp. 159 ff.; the whole of c. VI of this book on the art which flourished under the Mongol dynasty is interesting. See also L. Binyon, *Painting in the Far East* (1908), pp. 75–7, 146–7. One of Chao Mêng-fu's horse pictures, or rather a copy of it by a Japanese artist, is reproduced in Giles, *op. cit.*, opposite p. 159. See also my notes on illustrations for an account of the famous landscape roll painted by him in the style of Wang Wei.

[25] Bushell, *op. cit.*, p. 135.

[26] *Ib.*, pp. 135–6, where the picture is reproduced.

[27] For the episode of the mangonels constructed by Nestorian mechanics under the directions of Nicolo and Maffeo
see Marco Polo, *op. cit.*, pp. 281–2.

[28] Marco Polo, *op. cit.*, bk. III, c. I, pp. 321–3.

[29] Ramusio's preface, containing this account, and also the
story of how Rusticiano came to write the book at Marco
Polo's dictation at Genoa, is translated in Yule, *op. cit.*, I,
Introd., pp. 4–8.

[30] He mentions these in Marco Polo, *op. cit.*, pp. 136, 138,
344.

[31] Yule, *op. cit.*, I, Introd., p. 79.

[32] On Rusticiano (who is mistakenly called a Genoese by
Ramusio), see *ib.*, Introd., pp. 56 ff.

[33] Paulin Paris, quoted *ib.*, Introd., p. 61.

[34] *Ib.*, Introd., pp. 67–73.

[35] Extract from Jacopo of Acqui's *Imago Mondi*, quoted
ib., Introd., p. 54.

[36] M. Ch.-V. Langlois in *Hist. Litt. de la France*, XXXV
(1921), p. 259. For tributes to Marco Polo's accuracy see
Aurel Stein, *Ancient Khotan* (1907) and *Ruins of Desert
Cathay* (1912); Ellsworth Huntington, *The Pulse of Asia*
(1910); and Sven Hedin, *Overland to India* (1910).

[37] Yule, *op. cit.*, I, Introd., pp. 106–7.

[38] For these later missions and traders see Yule, *Cathay
and the Way Thither*, Introd., pp. cxxxii–iv, and text, *passim*.

[39] *Ib.*, II, p. 292; and App., p. lxv.

[40] Concerning the marginal notes by Columbus see Yule,
op. cit., II, App. H, p. 558. The book is preserved in the

Colombina at Seville. I must, however, frankly admit that modern research, iconoclastic as ever, not content with whitewashing Lucrezia Borgia and Catherine de Medicis, and with reducing Catherine of Siena to something near insignificance, is also making it appear more and more probable that Columbus originally set sail in 1492 to look for the islands of the Antilles, and that, although on his return after his great discovery in 1493 he maintained that his design had always been to reach Cipangu, this was a *post hoc* story, the idea of searching for Cipangu having probably come from his partner, Martin Pinzon. It is a pity that we do not know *when* he made his notes in the edition (the probable date of publication of which was 1485) of Marco Polo's book, which might settle the matter. On the whole question see Henry Vignaud, *Études critiques sur la vie de Colomb avant ses découvertes* (Paris, 1905) and *Histoire de la Grande Enterprise de 1492*, 2 vols. (Paris, 1910), and the summary and discussion of his conclusions by Professor A. P. Newton in *History*, VII (1922), pp. 38–42 (*Historical Revisions* XX.—"Christopher Columbus and his Great Enterprise.") The idea that a new road to the East was being sought at this time, primarily because the Turks were blocking the old trade routes, has also been exploded. See A. H. Lybyer, *The Ottoman Turks and the Routes of Oriental Trade* in Eng. Hist. Review, XXX (1915), pp. 577–88.

CHAPTER III

MADAME EGLENTYNE

A. RAW MATERIAL

1. Chaucer's description of the Prioress in the Prologue to the *Canterbury Tales*.

2. Miscellaneous visitation reports in episcopal registers. On these registers, and in particular the visitation documents therein, see R. C. Fowler, *Episcopal Registers of England and Wales* (S.P.C.K. Helps for Students of History, No. I), G. G. Coulton, *The Interpretation of Visitation Documents* (Eng. Hist. Review, 1914), and c. XII of my book, cited below. A great many registers have been, or are being, published by learned societies, notably by the Canterbury and York Society, which exists for this purpose. The most important are the Lincoln visitations, now in the course of publication, by Dr. A. Hamilton Thompson, *Visitations of Religious Houses in the Diocese of Lincoln*, ed. A. Hamilton Thompson (Lincoln Rec. Soc. and Canterbury and York Soc., 1915 ff.); two volumes have appeared so far, of which see especially vol. II, which contains part of Bishop Alnwick's visitations (1436–49); each volume contains text, translation, and an admirable introduction. See also the extracts from Winchester visitations trans. in H. G. D. Liveing, *Records of Romsey Abbey* (1912). Full extracts from visitation reports and injunctions are given under the accounts of religious houses in the different volumes of the Victoria County Histories (cited as V.C.H.).

3. The monastic rules. See *The Rule of St. Benedict*, ed. F. A. Gasquet (Kings Classics, 1909), and F. A. Gasquet, *English Monastic Life* (4th ed., 1910).

4. For a very full study of the whole subject of English convent life at this period see Eileen Power, *Medieval English Nunneries c. 1275 to 1535* (1922).

B. NOTES TO THE TEXT

[1] *The Register of Walter de Stapeldon, Bishop of Exeter* (1307–26), ed. F. Hingeston Randolph (1892), p. 169. The passage about Philippa is translated in G. G. Coulton, *Chaucer and His England* (1908), p. 181.

[2] See the account of expenses involved in making Elizabeth Sewardby a nun of Nunmonkton (1468) in *Testamenta Eboracensia*, ed. James Raine (Surtees Soc., 1886), III, p. 168; and Power, *op. cit.*, p. 19.

[3] *Year Book of King Richard II*, ed. C. F. Deiser (1904), pp. 71–7; and Power, *op. cit.*, pp. 36–8.

[4] G. J. Aungier, *Hist. of Syon* (1840), p. 385.

[5] As at Gracedieu (1440–1), *Alnwick's Visit*, ed. A. H. Thompson, pp. 120–3.

[6] G. J. Aungier, *op. cit.*, pp. 405–9.

[7] Translated from John de Grandisson's Register in G. G. Coulton, *A Medieval Garner* (1910), pp. 312–14.

[8] *Rule of St. Benedict*, c. 22.

[9] V. C. H. *Lincs.*, II, p. 131.

[10] Translated in G. G. Coulton, *A Medieval Garner*, p. 423.

[11] *Myroure of Oure Ladye*, ed. J. H. Blunt (E.E.T.S., 1873), p. 54. On Tittivillus see my article in *The Cambridge Magazine* (1917), pp. 158–60.

[12] *Linc. Visit.*, ed. A. H. Thompson, II, pp. 46–52; and Power, *op. cit.*, pp. 82–7.

[13] V. C. H. *Oxon*, II, p. 77.

[14] *Linc. Visit.*, ed. A. H. Thompson, I, p. 67.

[15] On these gaieties see Power, *op. cit.*, pp. 309–14.

16 *Linc. Visit.*, II, pp. 3–4; and see Power, *op. cit.*, pp. 75–7, 303–5, on gay clothes in nunneries.

17 *Linc. Visit.*, II, p. 175.

18 Power, *op. cit.*, p. 307. On pet animals see *ib.*, pp. 305–9, and Note E ("Convent Pets in Literature"), pp. 588–95.

19 Power, *op. cit.*, p. 77.

20 *Ib.* pp. 351–2; and see Chap. IX *passim* on the Bull *Periculoso* and the wandering of nuns in the world.

21 *Linc. Visit.*, II, p. 50.

22 V. C. H. *Yorks.*, III, p. 172.

CHAPTER IV

THE MÉNAGIER'S WIFE

A. RAW MATERIAL

1. *Le Ménagier de Paris, Traité de Morale et d'Economie Domestique, composé vers 1393 par un Bourgeois Parisien . . . publié pour la première fois par la Société des Bibliophiles Francois* (Paris, 1846). 2 vols., edited with an introduction by Jérôme Pichon. There is a notice of it by Dr. F. J. Furnivall, at the end of his edition of *A Booke of Precedence* (Early English Text Soc., 1869 and 1898), pp. 149–54. It was a book after his own heart, and he observes that it well deserves translation into English. I hope to publish in the not too distant future a slightly abbreviated translation, probably omitting the tales of *Mellibée et Prudence* and of *Griselda* and the poem *Le Chemin de Povreté et de Richesse*, which are not the Ménagier's own work.

2. On the subject of medieval books of deportment for women see A. A. Hentsch, *De la littérature didactique du moyen âge s'addressant spécialement aux femmes* (Cahors, 1903), an admirably complete collection of analyses of all the chief works of this sort produced in Western Europe from the time of St. Jerome to the eve of the Renaissance. It is full of plums for adventurous Jack Horners.

3. With the Ménagier's cookery book there may profitably be compared *Two Fifteenth Century Cookery Books*, ed. by Thomas Austin (E.E.T.S., 1888).

B. NOTES TO THE TEXT

[1] Pp. 1–2.

[2] These long moral treatises on the seven deadly sins and the even deadlier virtues were very popular in the Middle Ages. The best known to English readers occurs in the *Parson's Tale* in Chaucer's *Canterbury Tales*, and is taken from the *Somme*

de Vices et de Vertus of Frère Lorens, a thirteenth-century
author. The sections on the deadly sins are usually, however,
well worth reading, because of the vivid illustrative details
which they often give about daily life. The Ménagier's sections
are full of vigour and colour, as one would expect. Here, for
instance, is his description of the female glutton: "God com-
mands fasting and the glutton says: 'I will eat.' God com-
mands us to get up early and go to church and the glutton
says: 'I must sleep. I was drunk yesterday. The church is not
a hare; it will wait for me.' When she has with some difficulty
risen, do you know what her hours are? Her matins are: 'Ha!
what shall we have to drink? is there nothing left over from last
night?' Afterwards says she her lauds thus: 'Ha! we drank
good wine yesterday.' Afterwards she says thus her orisons:
'My head aches, I shan't be comfortable until I have had a
drink.' Certes, such gluttony putteth a woman to shame, for
from it she becomes a ribald, a disreputable person and a
thief. The tavern is the Devil's church, where his disciples go
to do him service and where he works his miracles. For when
folk go there they go upright and well spoken, wise and sensi-
ble and well advised, and when they return they cannot hold
themselves upright nor speak; they are all foolish and all mad,
and they return swearing, beating and giving the lie to each
other."—*Op. cit.*, I, pp. 47–8. The section on Avarice is particularly valuable for its picture of the sins of executors of wills,
rack-renting lords, extortionate shopkeepers, false lawyers,
usurers, and gamblers.—See *ib.*, I, pp. 44–5.

[3] *Prudence and Melibeus* is worth reading once, either in
Chaucer's or in Renault de Louens' version, because of its
great popularity in the Middle Ages, and because of occasional
vivid passages. Here, for instance, is the episode in Chaucer's
version, in which Melibeus, the sages, and the young men
discuss going to war, and the sages advise against it: "Up
stirten thanne the yonge folk at ones, and the mooste partie
of that compaignye scorned the wise olde men, and bigonnen
to make noyse, and seyden that 'Right so as, whil that iren is
hoot, men sholden smyte, right so men sholde wreken hir

wronges while that they been fresshe and newe'; and with
loud voys they criden, 'Werre! werre!' Up roos tho oon of
thise olde wise, and with his hand made contenaunce that men
sholde holden hem stille, and yeven hym audience.
'Lordynges,' quod he, 'ther is ful many a man that crieth
'Werre! werre!' that woot ful litel what werre amounteth.
Werre at his bigynnyng hath so greet an entryng and so large,
that every wight may entre whan hym liketh and lightly fynde
werre; but certes, what ende that shal ther-of bifalle it is nat
light to knowe; for soothly, whan that werre is ones bigonne
ther is ful many a child unborn of his mooder that shal sterve
yong by cause of that ilke werre, or elles lyve in sarwe, and dye
in wrecchednesse; and therfore, er that any werre bigynne, men
moste have greet conseil and greet deliberacioun."—Chaucer,
Tale of Melibeus, § 12; and see the French version, *op. cit.*, I,
p. 191.

[4] II, p. 72–9.

[5] I, pp. 71–2. These medieval games are very difficult to
identify. The learned editor remarks that *bric*, which is mentioned in the thirteenth century by Rutebeuf was played,
seated, with a little stick; *qui féry* is probably the modern
game called by the French *main chaude*; *pince merille*, which
is mentioned among the games of Gargantua, was a game in
which you pinched one of the players' arms, crying "Mérille"
or "Morille." Though the details of these games are vague,
there are many analagous games played by children to-day,
and it is easy to guess the kind of thing which is meant.

[6] I, pp. 13–15.

[7] I, 92, 96.

[8] The story of Jeanne la Quentine is reproduced in the
Heptameron of Margaret of Navarre (the 38th tale, or the
8th of the 4th day), where it is attributed to a *bourgeoise* of
Tours, but it is probable that the Ménagier's is the original
version, since he says that he had it from his father; although,

knowing the ways of the professional raconteur, I should be the
first to admit that this is not proof positive.

[9] I, pp. 125–6.

[10] I, p. 139.

[11] This was a favourite saying. It occurs in the story of
Melibeus, "Trois choses sont qui gettent homme hors de sa
maison, c'est assavoir la fumée, la goutière et la femme
mauvaise."—*Ib.*, I, p. 195. Compare Chaucer's use of it: "Men
seyn that thre thynges dryven a man out of his hous,—that is
to seyn, smoke, droppyng of reyn and wikked wyves."—*Tale
of Melibeus*, § 15; and

> "Thou seyst that droppyng houses, and eek smoke,
> And chidyng wyves, maken men to flee
> Out of hir owene hous."
>
> —*Wife of Bath's Prologue*, ll. 270–80.

[12] I, pp. 168–71, 174–6.

[13] II, p. 54. The Ménagier also warns against running up
long bills on credit. "Tell your folk to deal with peaceable
people and to bargain always beforehand and to account and
pay often, without running up long bills on credit by tally or
on paper, although tally or paper are better than doing everything by memory, for the creditors always think it more and
the debtors less, and thus are born arguments, hatreds, and
reproaches; and cause your good creditors to be paid willingly
and frequently what is owed to them, and keep them in friendship so that they depart not from you, for one cannot always
get peaceable folk again."

[14] II, pp. 56–9.

[15] It is curious here to note the antiquity of the term
"bloody" as an expletive. The Ménagier says: "Forbid them
. . . to use ugly oaths, or words which are bad or indecent, as
do certain evil or ill bred persons who swear at bad bloody
fevers, the bad bloody week, the bad bloody day ("de males

sanglantes fièvres," "de male sanglante sepmaine," "de male sanglante journée"), and they know not, nor should they know, what a bloody thing is, for honest women know it not, since it is abominable to them to see the blood but of a lamb or a pigeon, when it is killed before them."—*Ib.*, II, p. 59.

16 The section on household management described above occupies sec. II, art. 2, of the Ménagier's book (II, pp. 53–72).

17 I, pp. 171–2.

18 I, pp. 172–3.

19 The cookery book occupies sec. II, arts. 4 and 5 (II, pp. 80–272).

20 II, pp. 222–3. Translated by Dr. Furnivall in A *Booke of Precedence* (E.E.T.S.), pp. 152–3.

21 II, pp. 108–18, 123. The feast was still a thing of the future when the Ménagier thus gathered all the details. He calls it "L'ordenance de nopces que fera maistre Helye en May, á un mardy . . . l'ordonnance du souper que fera ce jour."

22 "The office of the women is to make provision of tapestries, to order and spread them, and in especial to dight the room and the bed which shall be blessed. . . . And *nota* that if the bed be covered with cloth, there is needed a fur coverlet of small vair, but if it be covered with serge, or broidery, or pinwork of cendal, not."—II, p. 118. The editor quotes the following ceremony for blessing the wedding bed: "*Benedictio thalami ad nuptias et als.* Benedic, Domine, thalamum hunc et omnes habitantes in eo, ut in tua voluntate permaneant, requiescant et multiplicentur in longitudinem dierum. Per Christum, etc. *Tunc thurificet thalamum in matrimonio, postea sponsum et sponsam sedentes vel jacentes in lecto suo. Benedicentur dicendo*: Benedic, Domine, adolescentulos istos; sicut benedixisti Thobiam et Sarram filiam Raguelis, ita benedicere eos digneris, Domine, ut in nomine tui vivant et senescant, et multiplicentur in longitudinem dierum. Per

Christum, etc. Benedictio Dei omnipotentis, Patris et Filii et
Spiritus sancti descendat super vos et maneat super vobiscum.
In nomine Patris, etc."—*Ib.*, I, *Introd.*, p. lxxxvi.

[23] Chaucer, *Tale of Melibeus*, § 15.

CHAPTER V

THOMAS BETSON

A. Raw Material

1. *The Stonor Letters and Papers, 1290–1483*, ed. C. L. Kingsford (Royal Hist. Soc., Camden, 3rd series), 2 vols., 1919. The Betson correspondence is in vol. II.

2. *The Cely Papers, selected from the Correspondence and Memoranda of the Cely Family, Merchants of the Staple, 1475–88*, ed. H. E. Malden (Royal Hist. Soc., Camden 3rd series), 1900.

I am much beholden to the excellent introductions to these two books, which are models of what editorial introductions should be.

3. The best introduction to the history of the Company of the Staple is to be found in Mr. Malden's aforesaid introduction to *The Cely Papers*, which also contains a masterly account of the political relations of England, France and Burgundy during the period. I have constantly relied upon Mr. Malden's account of the working of the Staple system. Other useful short accounts of the wool trade and the Stapler's Company may be found in the following works: Sir C. P. Lucas, *The Beginnings of English Overseas Enterprise* (1917), c. II; and A. L. Jenckes, *The Staple of England* (1908).

B. Notes to the Text

[1] Four interesting contemporary illustrations of Parliament in 1523, 1585, some date during the seventeenth century, and 1742 respectively, are reproduced in Professor A. F. Pollard's stimulating study of *The Evolution of Parliament* (1920).

[2] *The Lybelle of Englysshe Polycye*, in *Political Poems and Songs*, ed. Thos. Wright (Rolls Ser., 1861), II, p. 162. This remarkable poem was written in 1436 or 1437, in order to exhort the English "to kepe the see enviroun and namelye

the narowe see" between Dover and Calais, since in the author's opinion the basis of England's greatness lay in her trade, for the preservation of which she needed the dominion of the seas. Its chief value lies in the very complete picture which it gives of English import and export trade with the various European countries. There is a convenient edition of it in *The Principal Navigations Voyages Traffiques and Discoveries of the English Nation by Richard Hakluyt* (Everyman's Lib. Edition, 1907), I, pp. 174–202.

[3] G. W. Morris and L. S. Wood, *The Golden Fleece* (1922), p. 17.

[4] For accounts of these brasses see H. Druitt, *A Manual of Costume as Illustrated by Monumental Brasses* (1906), pp. 9, 201, 205, 207, 253. John Fortey's brass and William Greville's brass are conveniently reproduced in G. W. Morris and L. S. Wood, *op. cit.*, pp. 28, 32, together with several other illustrations, pertinent to the wool trade.

[5] Gower, *Mirour de l'Omme* in *The Works of John Gower.* I. *The French Works*, ed. G. C. Macaulay (1899), pp. 280–1.

[6] *The Paston Letters*, ed. J. Gairdner (London, 1872–5. Supplement 1901). See also H. S. Bennett, *The Pastons and their England* (1922).

[7] *Plumpton Correspondence*, ed. T. Stapleton (Camden Soc., 1839).

[8] *Cely Papers*, p. 72; and compare below p. 134.

[9] *Stonor Letters*, II p. 2.

[10] *Ib.*, II, pp. 2–3.

[11] The brasses of his father "John Lyndewode, woolman," and of his brother, also "John Lyndewode, woolman" (*d*.1421), are still in Linwood Church. They both have their feet on woolpacks, and on the son's woolpack is his merchant's mark. See H. Druitt, *op. cit.*, pp. 204–5.

[12] See *Magna Vita S. Hugonis Episcopi Lincolniensis*, ed. J. F. Dimock (Rolls Series, 1864), pp. 170–7.

[13] For these extracts see a vastly entertaining book, *Child Marriages and Divorces in the Diocese of Chester*, 1561–6, ed. F. J. Furnivall (E.E.T.S., 1897), pp. xxii, 6, 45–7.

[14] *Stonor Letters*, II, pp. 6–8.

[15] *Ib.*, II, pp. 28, 64.

[16] *Ib.*, II, p. 64.

[17] *Ib.*, II, pp. 42–43.

[18] *Ib.*, II, p. 44.

[19] *Ib.*, II, pp. 61, 64–5.

[20] *Ib.*, II, pp. 46–8.

[21] *Ib.*, II, p. 53.

[22] *Ib.*, II, p. 28.

[23] *Ib.*, II, p. 47.

[24] *Ib.*, II, p. 53.

[25] *Ib.*, II, pp. 54–5.

[26] *Ib.*, II, pp. 56–7.

[27] *Ib.*, II, p. 69.

[28] *Ib.*, II, pp. 87–8.

[29] *Ib.*, II, pp. 88–9.

[30] *Ib.*, II, p. 89.

[31] *Ib.*, II, pp. 102–3, 117.

[32] See Richard Cely's amusing account of the affair in a letter to his brother George, written on May 13, 1482, *Cely Papers*, pp. 101–4. For other references to the wool dealer

William Midwinter see *ib.*, pp. 11, 21, 28, 30, 32, 64, 87, 89, 90, 105, 124, 128, 157, 158.

[33] *Stonor Letters*, II, p. 3.

[34] *Ib.*, II, p. 64.

[35] *Testamenta Eboracensia* (Surtees Soc.), II, p. 56. He was a well-known wool merchant of York, at different times member of the town council of twelve, sheriff and mayor, who died in 1435. He is constantly mentioned in the city records; see *York Memorandum Book*, ed. Maud Sellers (Surtees Soc., 1912 and 1915), vols. I and II, *passim*.

[36] *Cely Papers*, pp. 30–1.

[37] *Ib.*, p. 64.

[38] See his will (1490) in *Test. Ebor.*, IV, p. 61, where he is called "Johannes Barton de Holme juxta Newarke, Stapulæ villæ Carlisiæ marcator," and ordains "Volo quod Thomas filius meus Johannem Tamworth fieri faciat liberum hominem Stapulæ Carlis," *ib.*, p. 62.

[39] *Ib.*, p. 45.

[40] *Ib.*, p. 48.

[41] *Ib.*, pp. 154–5.

[42] *The Lybelle of Englysshe Polycye* in *loc. cit.*, pp. 174–7, *passim*. Compare Gower's account of the machinations of the Lombards, *op. cit.*, pp. 281–2.

[43] See the clear account of all these operations in Mr. Malden's introduction to the *Cely Papers*, pp. xi–xiii, xxxviii.

[44] *Ib.*, p. vii.

[45] *Cely Papers*, pp. 194–6; and see *Introd.*, pp. xxxvi–viii.

[46] *Ib.*, pp. 71–2.

[47] *Ib.*, pp. 174–88, a book entitled on the cover "The Rekenyng of the Margett Cely," and beginning, "The first viage

of the Margaret of London was to Seland in the yere of our Lord God m iiij^{c}iiij^{xx}v. The secunde to Caleis and the thrid to Burdews ut videt. M^d to se the pursers accomptes of the seide viages. G. Cely."

[48] *Ib.*, p. xxxviii.

[49] *Stonor Letters,* II, p. 2.

[50] *Ib.*, II, p. 4.

[51] *Cely Papers,* pp. 112–13.

[52] *Ib.*, p. 106; compare *ib.*, p. 135.

[53] "Sir, the wool ships be come to Calais all save three, whereof two be in Sandwich haven and one is at Ostend, and he hath cast over all his wool overboard."—*Ib.*, p. 129. "Item, sir, on Friday the 27 day of February came passage from Dover and they say that on Thursday afore came forth a passenger from Dover to Calais ward and she was chased with Frenchmen and driven in to Dunkirk haven."—*Ib.*, p. 142. (There are many records of similar chases; see *Introd.*, pp. xxxiv–v.)

[54] *Ib.*, p. 135.

[55] "Sir, I cannot have your wool yet awarded, for I have do cast out a sarpler, the which is [ap]pointed by the lieutenant to be casten out toward the sort by, as the ordinance now is made that the lieutenant shall [ap]point the [a]warding sarplers of every man's wool, the which sarpler that I have casten out is No. 24, and therein is found by William Smith, packer, a 60 middle fleeces and it is a very gruff wool; and so I have caused William Smith privily to cast out another sarpler No. 8, and packed up the wool of the first sarpler in the sarpler of No. 8, for this last sarpler is fair wool enough, and therefore I must understand how many be of that sort and the number of the[m], for they must be packed again" (12 Sept., 1487).—*Ib.*, p. 160. "Item, sir, your wool is awarded by the sarpler that I cast out last, etc. Item, sir, this same day your mastership is elected and appointed here by the Court

one of the 28, the which shall assist the Master of the Staple now at this parliament time."—*Ib.*, p. 162.

56 Gower, *op. cit.*, p. 281.

57 *Cely Papers*, pp. xii, xxiv–v.

58 *Stonor Letters*, II, pp. 62–3; see also *Cely Papers*, pp. 1, 10, 13.

59 *Stonor Letters*, II, p. 4.

60 Chaucer, *Canterbury Tales* (*Shipman's Tale*) ll. 1243–6.

61 *Stonor Letters*, II, p. 48.

62 *Cely Papers*, p. xxiii.

63 *Lybelle of Englysshe Polycye* in *loc. cit.*, pp. 179–81.

64 With deference, I think that Mr. Malden in his introduction to the *Cely Papers*, App. II, pp. lii–iii, is mistaken in seeking to identify Synchon Mart with a particular fair at Antwerp on St. John's Day, Bammes mart with the fair at St. Rémy (a Flemish name for whom is Bamis) on August 8th, and Cold Mart with Cortemarck near Thourout. The names simply refer to the seasons in which there were fairs in most of the important centres, though doubtless in one place the winter and in another the spring, summer, or autumn fair was the more important. That the names refer to seasons and not to places appears quite clearly in various letters and regulations relating to the Merchant Adventurers of York. See *The York Mercers and Merchant Adventurers*, 1356–1917, ed. M. Sellers (Surtees Soc., 1918), pp. 117, 121–5, 147, 160, 170–1; see Miss Sellers' note, *ib.*, p. 122, quoting W. Cunningham: "The ancient Celti fairs . . . were a widespread primitive institution and appear to have been fixed for dates marked by the change of seasons."—*Scottish Hist. Review*, xiii, p. 168. For instance, a document of 1509 ("For now att this cold marte last past, holdyn at Barow in Brabond," *loc. cit.* p. 121) disposes of the idea that the Cold mart was the mart at Cortemarck, while another document refers to merchants intending

to ship "to the cold martes" and "to the synxon martes" in the plural. *Ib.*, p. 123. The identification of Balms mart with the fair at St. Rémy on August 8th is, moreover, belied by the same document (1510–11), which runs, "Whereas this present marte . . . we have lycensed and set you at libertie to shipp your commodities to the balmes marte next coming. Nevertheless . . . we thinke it good . . . that upon the recepte of these our letters ye . . . assemble and consult together, and if ye shall thinke good amongest yourselffs . . . discretly to withdraw and with holde your hands from shippyng to the said balmes marte. . . . Wryten at Andwarp the xvij day of August." *Ib.*, p. 124. The Balms mart was obviously the autumn fairtide, and Mr. Malden is no doubt right in identifying Balms (Bammys, Bammes) with Bamis, the local Flemish name of St. Rémy; St Rémy's Day was October 28th, and the Balms mart was not the mart held on August 8th at St Rémy, but the mart held on and round about St. Rémy's Day. Another document of 1552 gives interesting information about the shippings for three of the marts: "The last daye of shippinge unto the fyrst shippinge beinge for the pasche marte is ordeyned to be the laste of Marche nexte ensuyinge; and the seconde shippinge which is appointed for the sinxon marte the laste day to the same is appoynted the laste of June then nexte followinge; and unto the colde marte the laste day of shippinge is appoynted to be the laste of November then nexte insuyinge."–*Ib.*, p. 147. The Merchant Adventurers tried sometimes to restrict merchants to the Cold and the Synxon marts, which were the most important.

[65] *Cely Papers*, p. xl, and *passim*.

[66] *Ib.*, p. 74. Richard Cely the younger to George: "I understand that ye have a fair hawk. I am right glad of her, for I trust to God she shall make you and me right great sport. If I were sure at what passage ye would send her I would fetch her at Dover and keep her till ye come. A great infortune is fallen on your bitch, for she had 14 fair whelps, and after that she had whelped she would never eat meat, and so she is dead

and all her whelps; but I trust to purvey against your coming as fair and as good to please that gentleman."—*Ib.*, p. 74.

[67] *Ib.*, p. xlix.

[68] *Ib.*, App. I., pp. xlix–lii, a very interesting note on contemporary coinage, identifying all the coins mentioned in the letters.

[69] *Ib.*, p. 159.

[70] *Ib.*, p. 161.

[71] *Stonor Letters*, II, p. 43. So Dame Elizabeth Stonor ends a letter to her husband: "Written at Stonor, when I would fain have slept, the morrow after our Lady day in morning."—*Ib.*, p. 77.

[72] Chaucer, *Canterbury Tales* (*Shipman's Tale*), ll. 1265 –78, in *Works* (Globe Ed., 1903), p. 80.

[73] The will is P.C.C. 24 Logge at Somerset House. For this analysis of its contents and information about the life of Thomas Betson after his breach with the Stonors see *Stonor Letters*, I, pp. xxviii–ix.

[74] They are (1) John Bacon, citizen and woolman, and Joan, his wife (*d.* 1437); (2) Thomas Gilbert, citizen and draper of London and merchant of the Staple of Calais (*d.* 1483), and Agnes, his wife (*d.* 1489); (3) Christopher Rawson, mercer of London and merchant of the Staple of Calais, Junior Warden of the Mercers' Company in 1516 (*d.* 1518), and his two wives. Thomas Betson was doubtless acquainted with Gilbert and Rawson.

CHAPTER VI

THOMAS PAYCOCKE OF COGGESHALL

A. RAW MATERIAL

1. The raw material for this chapter consists of Paycocke's House, presented to the Nation in 1924 by the Right Hon. Noel Buxton, M.P., which stands in West Street, Coggeshall, Essex (station, Kelvedon); the Paycocke brasses, which lie in the North aisle of the parish church of St. Peter ad Vincula at Coggeshall; and the wills of John Paycocke (d. 1505), Thomas Paycocke (d. 1518), and Thomas Paycocke (d. 1580), which are now preserved at Somerset House (P.C.C. Adeane 5, Ayloffe 14, and Arundell 50, respectively), and of which that of the first Thomas has been printed in Mr. Beaumont's paper, cited below, while I have analysed fully the other two in my book, *The Paycockes of Coggeshall* (1920), which deals at length with the history of the Paycockes and their house. See also G. F. Beaumont, *Paycocke's House, Coggeshall, with some Notes on the Families of Paycocke and Buxton* (reprinted from Trans. Essex Archæol. Soc., IX, pt. V) and the same author's *History of Coggeshall* (1890). There is a beautifully illustrated article on the house in *Country Life* (June 30, 1923), vol. LIII, pp. 920–6.

2. For an apotheosis of the clothiers, see *The Pleasant History of John Winchcomb, in his younger days called Jack of Newbery, the famous and worthy Clothier of England* and *Thomas of Reading, or the Six Worthy Yeomen of the West*, in *The Works of Thomas Deloney*, ed. F. O. Mann (1912), nos. II and V. The first of these was published in 1597 and the other soon afterwards and both went through several editions by 1600.

3. On the cloth industry in general see G. Morris and L. Wood, *The Golden Fleece* (1922); E. Lipson, *The Woollen Industry* (1921); and W. J. Ashley, *Introd. to English Economic History* (1909 edit.). For the East Anglian woollen

industry see especially the *Victoria County Histories* of Essex and Suffolk. For a charming account of another famous family of clothiers see B. McClenaghan, *The Springs of Lavenham* (Harrison, Ipswich, 1924).

B. NOTES TO THE TEXT

[1] *Deloney's Works*, ed. F. O. Mann, p. 213.

[2] Thomas Fuller, *The Worthies of England* (1622), p. 318.

[3] A convenient introduction to the study of monumental brasses, with illustrations and a list of all the surviving brasses in England, arranged according to counties, is W. Macklin, *Monumental Brasses* (1913). See also H. Druitt, *Costume on Brasses* (1906). These books also give details as to the famous early writers on the subject, such as Weaver, Holman, and A.J. Dunkin.

[4] *Testamenta Eboracensia, a selection of wills from the Registry at York*, ed. James Raine, 6 vols. (Surtees Soc., 1836–1902). The Surtees Society has also published several other collections of wills from Durham and elsewhere, relating to the northern counties. A large number of wills have been printed or abstracted. See, for instance, *Wills and Inventories from the Registers of Bury St. Edmunds*, ed. S. Tymms (Camden Soc., 1850); *Calendar of Wills Proved and Enrolled in the Court of Hastings, London*, ed. R. R. Sharpe, 2 vols. (1889); *The Fifty Earliest English Wills in the Court of Probate, London*, ed. F. J. Furnivall (E.E.T.S., 1882); *Lincoln Wills*, ed. C. W. Foster (Lincoln Record Soc., 1914); and *Somerset Medieval Wills*, 1383–1558, ed. F. W. Weaver, 3 vols. (Somerset Record Soc., 1901–5).

[5] The will of the other Thomas Paycocke "cloathemaker," who died in 1580, also refers to the family business. He leaves twenty shillings "to William Gyon my weaver"; also "Item, I doe give seaven poundes tenne shillinges of Lawful money of Englande to and amongst thirtie of the poorest Journeymen of the Fullers occupacion in Coggeshall aforesaide, that

is to everye one of them fyve shillinges." William Gyon or
Guyon was related to a very rich clothier, Thomas Guyon,
baptized in 1592 and buried in 1664, who is said to have
amassed £100,000 by the trade. Thomas Paycocke's son-in-
law Thomas Tyll also came of a family of clothiers, for in a
certificate under date 1577 of wool bought by clothiers of
Coggeshall during the past year there occur the names of
Thomas Tyll, William Gyon, John Gooddaye (to whose family
the first Thomas Paycocke left legacies), Robert Lytherland
(who receives a considerable legacy under the will of the
second Thomas), and Robert Jegon (who is mentioned incidentally in the will as having a house near the church and was
father of the Bishop of Norwich of that name). See Power,
The Paycockes of Coggeshall, pp. 33–4.

[6] Quoted in Lipson, *Introd. to the Econ. Hist. of England*
(1905), I, p. 421.

[7] Quoted *ibid.*, p. 417.

[8] On John Winchcombe see Power, *op. cit.*, pp. 17–18; and
Lipson, *op. cit.*, p. 419.

[9] *Deloney's Works*, ed. F. O. Mann, pp. 20–1.

[10] *Ib.*, p. 22.

[11] Quoted in C. L. Powell, *Eng. Domestic Relations*, 1487–
1563 (1917), p. 27.

[12] The house subsequently passed, it is not quite clear at
what date, into the hands of another family of clothiers, the
Buxtons, who had intermarried with the Paycockes some time
before 1537. William Buxton (d. 1625) describes himself as
"clothyer of Coggeshall" and leaves "all my Baey Lombs
[Looms]" to his son Thomas. Thomas was seventeen when his
father died and lived until 1647, also carrying on business as a
clothier, and the house was certainly in his possession. He or
his father may have bought it from John Paycocke's executors.
By him it was handed down to his son Thomas, also a clothier
(d. 1713), who passed it on to his son Isaac, clothier (d.

1732). Isaac's two eldest sons were clothiers likewise, but soon after their father's death they retired from business. He apparently allowed his third son, John, to occupy the house as his tenant, and John was still living there in 1740. But Isaac had left the house by will in 1732 to his youngest son, Samuel, and Samuel, dying in 1737, left it to his brother Charles, the fourth son of Isaac. Charles never lived in it, because he spent most of his life in the pursuit of his business as an oil merchant in London, though he is buried among his ancestors in Coggeshall Church. In 1746 he sold the house to Robert Ludgater and it passed completely out of the Paycocke-Buxton connexion, and in the course of time fell upon evil days and was turned into two cottages, the beautiful ceilings being plastered over. It was on the verge of being destroyed some years ago when it was bought and restored to its present fine condition by Mr. Noel Buxton, a direct lineal descendant of the Charles Buxton who sold it. See Power, *op. cit.*, pp. 38–40.

[13] *Deloney's Works*, ed. F. O. Mann, p. 213.

[14] Defoe, *Tour through Great Britain*, 1724 (1769 edit.), pp. 144–6.

[15] "This shire is the most fatt, frutefull and full of profitable thinges, exceeding (as far as I can finde) anie other shire for the generall commodities and the plentie, thowgh Suffolk be more highlie comended by some (wherewith I am not yet acquainted). But this shire seemeth to me to deserve the title of the Englishe Goshen, the fattest of the lande, comparable to Palestina, that flowed with milk and hunnye."—Norden, *Description of Essex* (1594), (Camden Soc.), p. 7.

[16] According to Leake, writing about 1577, "About 1528 began the first spinning on the distaffe and making of Coxall clothes. . . . These Coxall clothes weare first taught by one Bonvise, an Italian."—Quoted V. C. H. *Essex*, II, p. 382.

INDEX

ANCHOR BOOKS

HISTORY

ADAMS, HENRY Mont-Saint-Michel and Chartres, A166
ALBRIGHT, W. F. From the Stone Age to Christianity, A100
BARK, WILLIAM CARROLL Origins of the Medieval World, A190
BARZUN, JACQUES Darwin, Marx, Wagner, A127
BURCKHARDT, JACOB The Age of Constantine the Great, A65
CABLE, GEORGE W. The Negro Question, A144
CASTIGLIONE, BALDESAR The Book of the Courtier, A186. Translated
 by Charles S. Singleton
COULANGES, FUSTEL DE The Ancient City, A76
FLORNOY, BERTRAND The World of the Inca, A137
FRANKFORT, HENRI The Birth of Civilization in the Near East, A89
GALILEO Discoveries and Opinions of, A94
GONCOURT, EDMUND and JULES DE The Goncourt Journals, A158
HADAS, MOSES, ed. A History of Rome, A78
HUIZINGA, J. The Waning of the Middle Ages, A42
KRAMER, SAMUEL NOAH History Begins at Sumer, A175
LEWIS, D. B. WYNDHAM François Villon, A147
LEWIS, W. H. The Splendid Century, A122
MATTINGLY, HAROLD Roman Imperial Civilisation, A160
MEYERHOFF, HANS, ed. The Philosophy of History in Our Time, A164
NEALE, J. E. Queen Elizabeth I, A105
NEHRU, JAWAHARLAL The Discovery of India, A200. Edited by Robert
 I. Crane
PIERSON, GEORGE W. and LUNT, DUDLEY C. Tocqueville in America,
 A189
PIRENNE, HENRI A History of Europe, 2 volumes, A156a, A156b
————— Medieval Cities, A82
POWER, EILEEN Medieval People, A32
SCOTT, GEOFFREY The Architecture of Humanism, A33
SIGERIST, HENRY The Great Doctors, A140
STEEGMULLER, FRANCIS The Grand Mademoiselle, A205
SYPHER, WYLIE Four Stages of Renaissance Style, A45
TOCQUEVILLE, ALEXIS DE The European Revolution and Correspond-
 ence with Gobineau, A163
————— The Old Regime and the French Revolution, A60
TREVELYAN, G. M. History of England, 3 volumes, A22a, A22b, A22c
TROTSKY, LEON The Russian Revolution, A170. Edited by F. W. Dupee
WADDELL, HELEN The Wandering Scholars, A63
WILLEY, BASIL The Seventeenth Century Background, A19
WILSON, EDMUND To the Finland Station, A6
WOODWARD, C. VANN Reunion and Reaction, A83

MUSIC

BARZUN, JACQUES Darwin, Marx, Wagner, A127
GREENBERG, NOAH, AUDEN, W. H. and KALLMAN, CHESTER An
 Elizabethan Song Book, A56
HAGGIN, B. H. The Listener's Musical Companion, A183
SHAW, BERNARD Shaw on Music, A53
TURNER, W. J. Mozart: The Man and His Works, A24

PHILOSOPHY

RELIGION